A WRITING BOOK
English in Everyday Life
A Teacher's Resource Book
Second Edition

Tina Kasloff Carver
Sandra Douglas Fotinos
Christie Kay Olson

PRENTICE HALL REGENTS
A VIACOM COMPANY

Prentice Hall Regents
Upper Saddle River, New Jersey 07458

Development Editor: *Carol Callahan, Barbara Barysh*
Director of Production and Manufacturing: *Aliza Greenblatt*
Executive Managing Editor: *Dominick Mosco*

Electronic Production Editors: *Michelle LoGerfo, Carey Davies, Wendy Wolf*
Electronic Art Specialist: *Steven Greydanus*
Production Assistant: *Christine Lauricella*
Art Director: *Merle Krumper*
Manufacturing Manager: *Ray Keating*

Illustrators: *Andrew Lange, Michelle LoGerfo*

Dedicated to Alice Olson with our love and thanks

Printed in the United States
10 9 8 7 6 5 4 3 2 1

0-13-187972-3

Prentice-Hall International (UK) Limited, *London*
Prentice-Hall of Australia Pty. Limited, *Sydney*
Prentice-Hall Canada Inc., *Toronto*
Prentice-Hall Hispanoamericana, S.A., *Mexico*
Prentice-Hall of India Private Limited, *New Delhi*
Prentice-Hall of Japan, Inc., *Tokyo*
Simon & Schuster Asia Pte. Ltd., *Singapore*
Editora Prentice-Hall do Brasil, Ltda., *Rio de Janeiro*

CONTENTS

UNIT 1: HANDWRITING   1

UNIT 2: JOURNALS   19

UNIT 3: GREETINGS

29

UNIT 4: ADDRESSES AND POSTAL SERVICES 37

UNIT 5: NOTES AND MESSAGES   53

UNIT 6: INVITATIONS AND THANK-YOU NOTES   67

UNIT 7: HOME AND HEALTH — 79

UNIT 8: TRAVEL — 95

UNIT 9: MONEY, BANKING, AND CREDIT 109

UNIT 10: EMPLOYMENT 121

UNIT 11: BUSINESS WRITING 135

FLIP SIDES 147

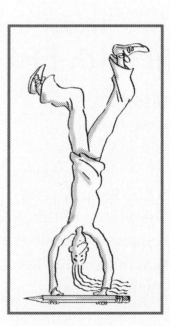

A CONVERSATION BOOK 1 Correlations

Units	AWB	ACB 1A	ACB 1B	ACB 1 Full
1. HANDWRITING	1			
Print with Uppercase Letters	2–4	3, 5, 33, 65	7, 36, 47, 65, 71, 78	3, 5, 33, 65, 97, 126, 137, 155, 161, 168
Print with Lowercase Letters	5-7	8, 17, 21, 26, 51, 53, 60, 67, 71	42-43	8, 17, 21, 26, 51, 53, 60, 67, 71, 132-133
Print with Upper and Lowercase Letters	8-9	2, 3, 7, 24, 31, 33, 40, 49, 55, 59, 65, 79, 80	xxviii, xxix, 7, 14, 9, 21, 23, 53, 55, 63, 67, 87, 89, 95, 100	2, 3, 7, 24, 31, 33, 40, 49, 55, 59, 65, 79, 80, 97, 104, 109, 111, 113, 143, 145, 153, 157, 177, 179, 185, 190
Write with Uppercase Letters	10-11	3, 5	xxviii, 7	3, 5, 97
Write with Lowercase Letters	12-15	8, 17, 21, 26, 51, 53, 60, 67, 71	42-43	8, 17, 21, 26, 51, 53, 60, 67, 71, 132-133
Write Your Signature	16	3, 31, 65	xxviii, 55, 67, 95	3, 31, 65, 145, 157, 185
Write Time Abbreviations	17	18-23, 67		18-23, 67
Write Dates	18	28-29, 32-33	55, 95	28-29, 32-33, 145, 185
2. JOURNALS	19			
Personal Information	20	2-7, 10-12, 65	xxviii-xxix	2-7, 10-12, 65
My Family	21	10-11		10-11
Today	22	16-21, 26-29		16-21, 26-29
In the Morning	23	17-23, 50		17-23, 50
Weather	24	36-38		36-38
Favorite Holiday	25	28-29, 32-33		28-29, 32-33
Thinking About Life	26	24, 27, 75-76	80-100	24, 27, 75-76, 170-190
Beliefs and Opinions	27	76-77	14, 25, 38-39, 50-51, 56-57, 73	76-77, 104, 115, 128-129, 140-141, 146-147, 163
A Day at Work	28	20-21	42-53	20-21, 132-143
3. GREETINGS	29			
Birthday Cards	30	30-31	10	30-31, 100
Valentines	31	32		32
Mother's Day Cards	32	10-11, 32-33		10-11, 32-33
Congratulations!	33		4-5, 10	94-95, 100
Thinking of You	34	62-63, 76-80	4-5, 10, 26-27, 50-53, 64-70, 74-77, 94-95	62-63, 76-80, 94-95, 100, 116-117, 140-143, 154-160, 164-167, 184-185
Get-Well Cards	35		10, 64-65, 68-71	100, 154-155, 158-161
Sympathy Cards	36		4-5, 10, 68-69	94-95, 100, 158-159
4. ADDRESSES AND POSTAL SERVICES	37			
Addresses	38	65		65
Abbreviations of Street Addresses	39	65		65
Ordinal Numbers	40-41	65		65
Abbreviations of States	42-43	65		65
Abbreviations of Titles	44	65		65
Addressing an Envelope	45-46		26-27	116-117
Envelopes with Special Instructions	47-48		26-27	116-117
Hold Mail	49		26-27, 94-95	116-117, 184-185
Change of Address	50-51	65	26-27	65, 116-117
Express Mail	52		26-27	116-117

A CONVERSATION BOOK 1 Correlations

Units	AWB	ACB 1A	ACB 1B	ACB 1 Full
5. NOTES AND MESSAGES	**53**			
Daily Planner	54	20-21, 26-29		20-21, 26-29
Notes to Yourself	55	20-21, 26-27, 58-59, 78-79, 82-83	6-7, 18-19, 26-29, 38-40, 66-67, 83	20-21, 26-27, 58-59, 78-79, 82-83, 96-97, 108-109, 116-119, 128-130, 156-157, 173
Telephone Messages	56-57	78-79	4-5, 20-23, 64-69	78-79, 94-95, 110-113, 154-159
Absence and Late Notes	58	14-15		14-15
Early Dismissal Notes	59	14-15	99	14-15, 189
Permission Slips	60		83, 98	173, 188
Notes to the Teacher	61	14-15	99	14-15, 189
Making Signs	62-63	14-15, 56-59	6, 10, 16-18, 30, 33, 47, 71	14-15, 56-59, 96, 100, 106-108, 120, 123, 137, 161
Notes for a Bulletin Board	64-65	14-15		14-15
Cancellation and Postponement Notices	66	36-38	91, 99	36-38, 181, 189
6. INVITATIONS & THANK-YOU NOTES	**67**			
Birthday Party Invitations	68	30–31	10	30-31, 100
Invite a Friend	69		20-21, 82-83	110-111, 172-173
Letter of Acceptance	70		82-83	172-173
Letter of Regret	71		82-83	172-173
Wedding Invitation	72	10	10, 82-83	10, 100, 172-173
Response to Formal Invitations	73-74	10	10, 82-83	10, 100, 172-173
Invitation to an Honored Guest	75		10	100
Thank-you Note for a Gift	76	30-33	10	30-33, 100
Thank-you Note for a Visit	77		10, 94-95	100, 184-185
Thank-you Note for Help	78	76-77	10	76-77, 100
7. HOME AND HEALTH	**79**			
Salad Recipes	80	44-45		44-45
Soup Recipes	81	44-47, 58-59		44-47, 58-59
Dessert Recipes	82	48-49		48-49
Menu Planning	83-84	42-60	63	42-60, 153
Supermarket Shopping List	85	58-59		58-59
Saving Money with Coupons	86	58-59		58-59
Comparison Shopping	87	58-59		58-59
Rental Agreement	88-89	62-65, 78-79		62-65, 78-79
Housing Complaint	90-91	78-79		78-79
Shopping for Home Repair Supplies	92	78-79	2, 9, 39-40	78-79, 92, 99, 129-130
Pharmacy Shopping	93		6-7, 64-65, 68-69	96-97, 154-155, 158-159
Health Insurance Form	94		56-57, 66-70	146-147, 156-160

A CONVERSATION BOOK 1 Correlations

Units	AWB	ACB 1A	ACB 1B	ACB 1 Full
8. TRAVEL	95			
Giving Directions	96	65	16-19, 31, 34, 36	65, 106-109, 121, 124, 126
Directions from School to Home	97	65	16-19	65, 106-109
Directions to the Library	98		18-19, 98	108-109, 188
Directions to the Park	99		18-19, 92-93	108-109, 182-183
Directions to the Hospital	100		18-19, 68-71	108-109, 158-161
Driver License Application	101-102		32-33	122-123
Geographic Regions	103	34-39, 62-63	94-97	34-39, 62-63, 184-187
Vacation Postcards	104	5, 62-63	94-97	5, 62-63, 184-187
Letters about a Visit	105-106	62-63	94-97	62-63, 184-187
Customs Declaration	107-108		94-95	184-185
9. MONEY, BANKING, AND CREDIT	109			
Writing Amounts of Money	110	49, 55, 59, 60, 91, 92	5, 7-11, 27-29	49, 55, 59, 60, 91, 92, 95, 97-101, 117-119
Writing Checks	111-112	91	28-29	91, 118-119
Recording Checks	113		28-29	118-119
Overdrawing an Account	114		28-29	118-119
Saving Money	115		28-29	118-119
Automated Teller Machine	116		28-29	118-119
Withdrawing Money	117		28-29	118-119
Credit Card Application	118-119	91		91
Credit Card Finance Charge	120	91		91
10. EMPLOYMENT	121			
Cover Letter	122		42-43, 54-55	132-133, 144-145
Résumé	123-124		54-55	144-145
Employment Application	125-126		42-43, 54-55	132-133, 144-145
Social Security Card	127			
Employee Withholding Allowance Certificate (W-4)	128-129		56-57	146-147
Request for Earnings and Benefit Estimate Statement	130		57	147
U.S. Income Tax Return	131-132			
Unemployment	133-134		52-53, 56-57	142-143, 146-147
11. BUSINESS WRITING	135			
Business Letter: Request for Information	136-137		18-19, 36	108-109, 126
College Information Request	138		98-99	188-189
Classified Ads	139		12-13	102-103
Car Ads	140		32-34	122-124
Mail Order	141	82-83, 90-92	2-3	82-83, 90-93
Returning Merchandise	142	82-92	2-14	82-104
Complaint about a Billing Error	143			
Free Offers	144			
Cancelling a Subscription	145			

A CONVERSATION BOOK 2 Correlations

Units	AWB	ACB 2A	ACB 2B	ACB 2 Full
1. HANDWRITING	1			
Print with Uppercase Letters	2-4			
Print with Lowercase Letters	5-7	27		27
Print with Upper and Lowercase Letters	8-9	8	xxii	8
Write with Uppercase Letters	10-11			
Write with Lowercase Letters	12-15	4, 8, 19, 29, 37, 39, 42, 49, 62, 65, 67, 73, 86	xxiii, 19, 27, 44-45, 49, 56, 69, 74, 85, 89, 96	4, 8, 19, 29, 37, 39, 42, 49, 62, 65, 67, 73, 86, 123, 131, 148-149, 153, 160, 173, 178, 189, 193, 200
Write Your Signature	16			
Write Time Abbreviations	17			
Write Dates	18			
2. JOURNALS	19			
Personal Information	20	2-9, 44-62		2-9, 44-62
My Family	21	32-37, 44-62		32-37, 44-62
Today	22	24-25, 28-29		24-25, 28-29
In the Morning	23	24-25, 28-29		24-25, 28-29
Weather	24	34-35, 84-85, 90-91	80-81	24-25, 84-85, 90-91, 184-185
Favorite Holiday	25			
Thinking About Life	26	28-29, 34-35, 38-39, 40-41, 84-85		28-29, 34-35, 38-39, 40-41, 84-85
Beliefs and Opinions	27	12-19, 24-25, 30-31, 34-35, 38-39, 48-61, 66-67, 78-79, 80-81, 88-89, 92-103	2-3, 18-21, 24-31, 46-55, 62-73, 82-83, 86-95	12-19, 24-25, 30-31, 34-35, 38-39, 48-61, 66-67, 78-79, 80-81, 88-89, 92-103, 106-107, 122-125, 128-135, 150-159, 166-177, 190-200, 186-187
A Day at Work	28		58-74	162-178
3. GREETINGS	29			
Birthday Cards	30	6-9, 70-71	76-77	6-9, 70-71, 180-181
Valentines	31	46-49	16-17	46-49, 120-121
Mother's Day Cards	32	44-45, 48-55, 60-61		44-45, 48-55, 60-61
Congratulations!	33	10-11, 46-51	20-21, 72-73, 76-77, 82-83, 94-95	10-11, 46-51, 124-125, 176-177, 180-181, 186-187, 198-199
Thinking of You	34	30-35, 20-21, 58-61, 70-71, 102-103	12-15, 32-35, 76-77, 80-81	20-21, 30-35, 58-61, 70-71, 102-103, 116-119, 136-139, 180-181, 184-185
Get-Well Cards	35	90-101	64-65	90-101, 168-169
Sympathy Cards	36	20-21, 60-61		20-21, 60-61
4. ADDRESSES AND POSTAL SERVICES	37			
Addresses	38	9, 64-67, 70-71, 74-75	50-51	9, 64-67, 70-71, 74-75, 154-155
Abbreviations of Street Addresses	39	9, 64-67, 70-71	50-51	9, 64-65, 70-71, 154-155

A CONVERSATION BOOK 2 Correlations

Units	AWB	ACB 2A	ACB 2B	ACB 2 Full
Ordinal Numbers	40-41	9, 70-71	50-51	9, 70-71, 154-155
Abbreviations of States	42-43	9, 70-71		9, 70-71
Abbreviations of Titles	44	9, 70-71		9, 70-71
Addressing an Envelope	45-46	70-71		70-71
Envelopes with Special Instructions	47-48	70-71		70-71
Hold Mail	49		32-40	136-143
Change of Address	50-51		14-15	118-119
Express Mail	52	70-71, 74-75		70-71, 74-75
5. NOTES AND MESSAGES	**53**			
Daily Planner	54	24-25, 88-89		24-25, 88-89
Notes to Yourself	55	24-25, 98-99	32-33, 52-53, 76-79	24-25, 98-99, 136-137, 156-157, 180-183
Telephone Messages	56-57	72-75, 94-95		72-75, 94-95
Absence and Late Notes	58	56-57, 80-81		56-57, 80-81
Early Dismissal Notes	59	56-57, 80-81		56-57, 80-81
Permission Slips	60	56-57, 80-81		56-57, 80-81
Notes to the Teacher	61	16-19, 56-57, 80-81	76-77	16-19, 74-75, 80-81, 180-181
Making Signs	62-63	76-77, 80-81	64-65	76-77, 80-81, 168-169
Notes for a Bulletin Board	64-65	16-19, 74-75, 80-81, 102-103	76-77	16-19, 74-75, 80-81, 102-103, 180-181
Cancellation and Postponement Notices	66	84-85	76-77, 80-81, 90-91	84-85, 180-181, 184-185, 194-195
6. INVITATIONS & THANK-YOU NOTES	**67**			
Birthday Party Invitations	68	6-9, 70-71	76-77	6-9, 70-71, 180-181
Invite a Friend	69		32-33	136-137
Letter of Acceptance	70		32-33	136-137
Letter of Regret	71		32-33	136-137
Wedding Invitation	72	46-47	76-77	46-47, 180-181
Formal Invitations, Acceptance, Regrets	73-74	48-49	76-77	48-49, 180-181
Invitation to an Honored Guest	75	102-103	94-95	102-103, 198-199
Thank-you Note for a Gift	76	10-11, 70-71		10-11, 70-71
Thank-you Note for a Visit	77		32-33	136-137
Thank-you Note for Help	78	16-19	94-95	16-19, 198-199
7. HOME AND HEALTH	**79**			
Salad Recipes	80	26-27, 88-89		26-27, 88-89
Soup Recipes	81	26-27, 88-89		26-27, 88-89
Dessert Recipes	82	26-27, 88-89		26-27, 88-89
Menu Planning	83-84	26-27, 88-89		26-27, 88-89
Supermarket Shopping List	85	26-27, 88-89		26-27, 88-89
Saving Money with Coupons	86		68-69	172-173
Comparison Shopping	87		68-69	172-173
Rental Agreement	88-89		2-15	106-119
Housing Complaint	90-91		8-11	112-115
Shopping for Home Repair Supplies	92		8-13, 20-21	112-117, 124-125
Pharmacy Shopping	93	92-93, 98-99		92-93, 98-99
Health Insurance Form	94	94-99		94-99

A CONVERSATION BOOK 2 Correlations

Units	AWB	ACB 2A	ACB 2B	ACB 2 Full
8. TRAVEL	95			
Giving Directions	96	64-67, 84-85		64-67, 84-85
Directions from School to Home	97	64-65		64-65
Directions to the Library	98	64-67		64-67
Directions to the Park	99	64-65, 84-85		64-65, 84-85
Directions to the Hospital	100	94-97		94-97
Driver License Application	101-102		26-29	130-133
Geographic Regions	103		32-39, 80-81	136-143, 184-185
Vacation Postcards	104		32-39	136-143
Letters about a Visit	105-106		32-39	136-143
Customs Declaration	107-108		32-39	136-143
9. MONEY, BANKING, AND CREDIT	109			
Writing Amounts of Money	110			
Writing Checks	111-112	76-77	8-9, 30-33, 68-69	76-77, 112-113, 134-137, 172-173
Recording Checks	113	76-77	8-9, 30-33, 68-69	76-77, 112-113, 134-137, 172-173
Overdrawing an Account	114		8-9, 68-69	112-113, 172-173
Saving Money	115	74-77, 82-83	30-33, 68-69	74-77, 82-83, 134-137, 172-173
Automated Teller Machine	116	76-77		76-77
Withdrawing Money	117	76-77	32-33, 68-69	76-77, 136-137, 172-173
Credit Card Application	118-119	74-77	30-33, 68-69	74-77, 134-137, 172-173
Credit Card Finance Charge	120	74-77	30-33, 68-69	74-77, 134-137, 172-173
10. EMPLOYMENT	121			
Cover Letter	122		42-53	146-157
Résumé	123-124		42-53	146-157
Employment Application	125-126		42-53	146-157
Social Security Card	127		42-55	146-159
Employee Withholding Allowance Certificate (W-4)	128-129		54-55, 66-67, 70-71	158-159, 170-171, 174-175
Request for Earnings and Benefit Estimate Statement	130		54-55, 66-67	158-159, 170-171
U.S. Income Tax Return	131-132		70-71	174-175
Unemployment Weekly Benefit Statement	133-134		72-73	176-177
11. BUSINESS WRITING	135			
Business Letter: Request for Information	136-137	84-85, 90-103	26-39	84-85, 90-103, 130-143
College Information Request	138	82-83		82-83
Classified Ads	139	74-77	6-7, 10-11	74-77, 110-111, 114-115
Car Ads	140	10	30-31	10, 134-135
Order by Mail	141	74-75		74-75
Returning Merchandise	142	78-79		78-79
Complaint about a Billing Error	143	78-79	8-9	78-79, 112-113
Free Offers	144	74-75		74-75
Cancelling a Subscription	145	78-79		78-79

TO THE TEACHER

SPECIAL FEATURES

Welcome to the Second Edition of *A WRITING BOOK!* There are four special features of this new edition:

- *A WRITING BOOK* is now a teacher's resource book of over one hundred everyday writing lessons with optional "flip sides" to be photocopied for classroom use. (See next page for a description of flip sides.)

- The writing tasks are cross-referenced to corresponding pages of our series *A CONVERSATION BOOK 1(Full Edition 1A/1B): English in Everyday Life, Third Edition* and *A CONVERSATION BOOK 2 (Full Edition 2A/2B): English in Everyday Life, Third Edition.*

- The writing tasks are all designed as interactive learning activities.

- An **Activities Guide** is included, with suggestions for teaching the individual activities.

PURPOSE AND CONTENT

Most ESL students are confronted with English writing tasks in their everyday lives before they are ready to handle them. Whether they need to fill out a driver license application, write an absence note for a child in school, or open a bank account, the problem is the same—the need to write in English arises very quickly in ESL students' lives. *A WRITING BOOK: English in Everyday Life, Second Edition* is designed to help meet this need.

A WRITING BOOK includes a wide variety of everyday writing tasks and the conventions associated with each task. New tasks have been added to reflect changes in technology and to encourage personal journal writing as a way of developing writing fluency. The activities provide concrete practice for everyday writing, such as filling in applications and other forms, addressing envelopes, improving printing and handwriting, and writing checks, notes, business letters, cards, lists, recipes, messages, announcements, and journals.

LEVELS

The activities provided will be useful for students of beginning to high intermediate levels of ESL ability. Since most everyday writing tasks are highly conventional, students do not need to know a great deal of English grammar to complete them. Many of the writing tasks in the book are broken into manageable segments and based on fill-in models to guide the students. Thus, even students with very limited English will be able to complete most tasks successfully.

LESSON DESIGN

Each lesson is either one or two pages long. It begins with a prewriting activity in which students can explore the ideas and vocabulary of the lesson. The main writing task follows and the lesson concludes with one or more expansion activities. It is recommended that all students have a notebook and divide it into sections: *Vocabulary, Journal, Community Information, and Activities*

FLIP SIDES

At the back of *A WRITING BOOK* is a set of ten variations of formatted blank pages to be used as optional flip sides for the lessons. Choose whichever format you find most useful for each lesson, and copy that flip side on the back of the lesson sheet. The formats include: *Business Letter, Directions, Journal, Letter, List, Listen and Write, Partner Interview, Personal Letter, Review, Vocabulary, Weekly Planner,* and a form without a title for whatever other expansion or reinforcement activity you wish to add. By using the flip sides, you can take advantage of the flexibility of this book and be "environmentally correct" at the same time by utilizing both sides of the photocopy paper!

CORRELATIONS TO A CONVERSATION BOOK

The writing lessons in this book are designed to be used as supplementary writing activities. The activities can be used together with any course book. They are also specifically appropriate expansion and reinforcement for the lessons in *A CONVERSATION BOOK, English in Everyday Life, 3rd Edition* series. Teachers who are using any of the *CONVERSATION BOOKS* with their classes will find will find it useful to consult the correlations in both a *A CONVERSATION BOOK* (in the Teacher's Guide) and *A WRITING BOOK* (in the front matter). The cross-referencing will help teachers coordinate their lessons.

SPELLING HINTS

On the title page of each unit is a "Spelling Hint," a basic spelling rule with examples, which may be presented and discussed with the whole class in any order and at any time. There are eleven Spelling Hints:

Unit 1: the **ch** sound

Unit 2: the **k** sound

Unit 3: plurals

Unit 4: silent **e**

Unit 5: doubling final consonants

Unit 6: the consonant plus **y** rule

Unit 7: the long **a** sound

Unit 8: the long **e** sound

Unit 9: the long **i** sound

Unit 10: the long **o** sound

Unit 11: the short **u** sound

ACTIVITIES GUIDE

All of the activities in *A WRITING BOOK, Second Edition* are student-centered and task-based, and all are designed to require real communication. The activities fall into four major groups: **Class Activities, Group Activities, Partner Activities,** and **Individual Activities.** This guide includes abbreviated suggestions for teaching each kind of activity.

Class Activities

Class Brainstorm

OBJECTIVE: To encourage students to think beyond bounds of right and wrong; to tap into students' prior knowledge about a topic and share useful information in written form.

- Explain the concept of "brainstorming" as allowing for the free flow of ideas without worrying about corrections or changes. Remind students that their suggestions will be listed quickly, without any discussion of the ideas generated.

- Select a student volunteer to record the suggestions on the board.

- Select another student volunteer to "be the teacher" and ask for ideas, keep order if everyone wants to talk at once, and make sure that all ideas are put on the board.

- If students have difficulty getting started, give them an example to begin the list.

- When the list is completed, have the student recorder read it aloud.

- Help students make any corrections or changes needed.

- Discuss any items on the list that may be especially appropriate.

- Have students copy the list in their notebooks or on the flip side of their handout.

Class Game

OBJECTIVE: To use prior knowledge in a variety of game formats for reinforcement.

- There are four **Class Games** in *A WRITING BOOK:* "**Guess Who?**," "**Respond**," "**Thank you!**" and "**Win a Wig! Win a Cruise!**"

- Explain the purpose and procedures of "**Guess Who?**" to the class. Demonstrate by putting several sample pieces of paper, each with a different task, on a desk or table, mixing them up, picking one up, and reading from it.

  - Have students write whatever is required (a journal entry, an invitation, the name of a gift, or your name).

  - Have students fold their papers and put them in a pile together.

  - Have a volunteer mix up the papers, then choose one and read it to the class.

  - At this point have the other students guess who wrote the paper. Then have the first volunteer choose another student to take a turn, and so on until everyone has taken a turn.

- In **"Respond"** have pairs of students write a telephone conversation in which they accept or decline an invitation from another pair. The partners role-play their decision to accept or not to accept the party invitation in a telephone conversation for the class with the partners who wrote the invitation. Then have another pair of students pick an invitation from the pile, and so on.

- In **"Thank you!"** have the student announce the gift written on the paper. The student who wrote that "gift" will be the next student to pick a "gift" from the pile, and so on. When everyone has picked a gift, have all students write thank-you notes for the gifts and read their notes aloud—either to the student who "sent" the gift or to the class.

- In **"Win a Wig! Win a Cruise!"** the student who picked the first name announces the winner of the wig. Then have another student pick a name for the winner of the cruise. As a variation, before the game begins, have students make a wig and draw a cruise picture or a "bon voyage" card for the actual prizes.

Class Project

OBJECTIVE: *To work together with the class on multiple tasks , including writing and planning, which result in a feeling of whole class accomplishment, building a sense of class identity, team spirit, and trust.*

- There are seven **Class Projects** in *A WRITING BOOK* : Making Signs for the Classroom, Making a Class Bulletin Board, Making a Class Recipe Book, Having a Class Party, Having a Class Yard Sale, Starting a Lending Library or Exchange, and Going on a Class Trip to a Park.

- Each of these projects will take more than one class period to complete.

- Three of them—the Classroom Signs, Bulletin Board, and Lending Library—may be continued throughout the semester.

- Three of them—the Class Party, Class Yard Sale, and Class Trip to a Park—involve planning for and carrying out a class event.

- One, the Class Recipe Book, involves compiling the writing of all or most of the students in the class.

- For each project, it is essential that all students understand their responsibilities for the success of the project.

- Brainstorm a list of tasks for the project and have a student recorder write the list on the board.

- Have students volunteer for the various tasks and write their names on the board next to their chosen task. Some tasks may be completed by one student; others may require groups.

- Have them copy the final list in their notebooks.

- If there are groups, give them class time to meet and prepare together.

- At every class session until the project is completed, review the tasks by having a student volunteer or each group report on the progress of the project.

- When the project is completed, have students write a journal entry about it.

Class Survey

OBJECTIVE: *To encourage students to voice opinions and preferences, to compare their preferences with those of classmates, and to check accuracy in recording answers.*

- Model the questions; have students repeat them; check pronunciation. If appropriate, add one more item together. Be sure students understand all the vocabulary and the objective of the activity before beginning the survey.

- If the survey is presented with columns to check off, have students check their own answers in the appropriate columns.

- If there are only survey questions listed on the page, have students write their own responses on the page.

- Instruct students to circulate and ask their classmates the questions. To vary the method, tell students to ask five or ten classmates the questions and write or check their responses.

- While the students are working, copy the questions on the board.

- Have students report their results to the class—or to a group. If they report to a group, have the group report to the class.

- When all students or groups have reported, ask students to guess what the total numbers for each choice—or total of each kind of response—will be for the class. Write guess totals next to the questions.

- Ask the whole class the questions. Have students raise their hands to show responses; count the raised hands. Then write the correct numbers on the board. See if anyone's guesses were right!

Community Activity

OBJECTIVE: *To broaden students' horizons through discovering uses of written English outside the classroom and to increase awareness and knowledge of community resources and services.*

- There are sixteen different kinds of **Community Activities** in *A WRITING BOOK.* Each of these activities has its own specific instructions, and the instructions vary considerably from one activity to another.

- All **Community Activities** involve some kind of active research, usually finding information outside of class and bringing it in to share and compare with the class.

- Since the results of this research—and the difficulties involved in carrying it out—will vary, depending on your community, we suggest that you try it yourself before assigning it to the students. Then you can forewarn them of problems they may encounter.

- For the activities that require group work outside of class, help students arrange to do the group work together. If that is not possible, adjust the instructions to allow them to complete the community tasks individually.

- Review the task before asking students to work independently. These tasks can be intimidating at first. Students who perform well in class may still worry about using English outside the classroom.

- To help prepare students, role-play possible conversations in English that may be required during the actual activity. If possible, the first time a community activity requires verbal interaction in the community, travel as a class to give the students confidence.

- In an EFL class, if need be, have students do the research in their first language and then translate it. Have students use the opportunity to explore where English is used in their own country and culture. This activity will give students an insight into how important the study of English is, even in the midst of their own familiar surroundings.

- Make sure that all students report back on the information they have gathered.

- Write the final results of the community research on the board, discuss the results as appropriate, and have students copy the results in their notebooks or on the flip side of their handout.

Cross-Cultural Exchange

OBJECTIVE: *To discuss as a whole class the practices or issues that are handled differently in different cultures or countries; to increase awareness of cultural diversity and the variety of individual experience and perceptions; to practice withholding judgment.*

- Some of the **Cross-Cultural Exchange** activities in *A WRITING BOOK* are written as whole class activities; others are written as group activities. The group **Cross-Cultural Exchanges** are for topics or situations about which many students may be expected to have had prior knowledge. Depending on the experience and prior knowledge of the students in your class, you may want to vary the format of a **Cross-Cultural Exchange** from group to whole-class discussions, or vice versa.

- Read al the questions together. Tell students to give as many answers as possible to every question. Their answers should be based on their own personal experiences.

- Explain the objective of the activity. Remind the students that everyone has different experiences and that in this activity it is important to try to understand differences rather than to judge them.Tell students to listen carefully, ask questions when they don't understand, and withhold judgements—avoid judging other students' experiences and customs.

- Appoint a volunteer recorder to write down all of the students' answers to each question.

- Ask the questions one by one, and encourage students to give as many answers as they can.

- Whenever possible, have students share stories or teach the class something interesting about their own culture. This validates students' backgrounds, fosters self-esteem, and is essential in building a student-centered classroom.

- At the end of the activity, help the class to summarize and compare the cultural information gathered.

Find Someone Who...

OBJECTIVE: *To encourage students to share personal information with classmates and to practice creating, asking, and answering "Yes/No questions."*

- Review the vocabulary in the activity, and add one or two more items if appropriate.

- Ask the students what "Yes/No questions" they will need to ask in order to complete the activity.

- Write the appropriate "Yes/No questions" on the board, or have a student volunteer write them.

- Practice asking and answering the "Yes/No questions" with the class. This is a good time to practice pronunciation and review grammar constructions as needed.

- Have students circulate around the classroom asking one another all the questions and writing down as many students' names corresponding to "yes" answers as they can.

- Remind students that they should write ONLY the names of students who say "yes" to a question.

- If the class is very large, divide students into groups of 10 to 15. Have students ask the questions within these smaller groups.

- Give the class a time limit of five or ten minutes.

- Tell students to be seated when they have finished asking and answering all the questions.

- At the end of the allotted time or when all students have finished—whichever comes first—ask the class or the groups for their results.

- Follow up on individual answers with appropriate questions. These should provide interesting springboards for story sharing and conversation!

Listen and Write

OBJECTIVE: *To write from the teacher's dictation as a means to reinforce the relationship between the oral and the written language and to practice listening and spelling vocabulary.*

- Have students write their names at the top of their papers.

- Explain that you will dictate individual words and that students need to write the words on their papers. Assure students that you will repeat the words as often as needed.

- Dictate the words one by one. Use clear but "normal" pronunciation—do not overstress or alter sounds from "normal" pronunciation.

- Ask the class if they would like you to repeat any of the words. Repeat as requested.

- When everyone has finished writing, have students exchange papers.

- Ask everyone in the class to spell the words back to you. As they spell each word, write the word on the board. If very few students are speaking, say, *"I can't hear you! Everyone, spell!"* If they spell a word wrong, or mispronounce a letter, write the misspelling or the mispronunciation. When you finish writing the word, ask, *"Is that right?"* Have students continue correcting the word until everyone agrees that it is correct.

- When each word is written correctly on the board, tell students to put a ✓ next to each correct word on their partner's paper or write the correct spelling if they see an error.

- When completed, tell students to add up the number correct and put it at the top of the paper.

- Have students return the papers to their partners. Ask which words the students had problems with. Discuss the problems.

- For more practice and reinforcement, dictate "problem" words or phrases again, and have students write them on the **Listen and Write** flip side of their handout.

Print with the Class

OBJECTIVE: *To practice printing legibly in appropriate situations with the class.*

- These activities appear in *Unit 1: Handwriting* for practice printing legibly and in later units where students need to print a class map and cancellation notice. *A WRITING BOOK* also includes many forms that require printing. The **Print** activities for these forms can often be completed individually. However, when a form is very complicated and difficult for your students, change the format of the activity to **Print with the Class.**

- Explain to students that there are many styles of printing, but that whatever style they use, their printing should always be clear and legible. Many forms require printing because the information must be filled in legibly!

- Have the class read the instructions for the activity aloud.

- If the lesson requires filling in a form, there is generally a **Read with the Class** activity first, in which students study the vocabulary, meaning, and information required on the form. Make sure all students understand all parts of the form before starting to fill it in. Then reread the form line by line and fill in each line together. Print sample fill-in answers on the board as needed.

- For other printing tasks, select a student volunteer to print on the board. Encourage everyone in the class to make suggestions for what to print. If students are reluctant, have everyone print one possibility on a small piece of paper and hand it in to you. Read the papers to the class, and have everyone select pieces to print on the board. When the printing task is complete, have everyone copy it from the board into their notebooks or onto the flip side of their handout.

- Discuss with the whole class any questions or problems that come up during the process.

Read with the Class

OBJECTIVE: *To clarify vocabulary, read, and discuss difficult forms and other writing models and to add more possible completions based on students' experience and interests; to read individual student's writing to the whole class.*

- Many of these activities are included to help students understand a form or other piece of writing which is above their normal reading level and which contains specialized, unfamiliar vocabulary. You may need to spend considerable time clarifying vocabulary and paraphrasing for the class. This is not a waste of time. Becoming familiar with such forms and developing the skills to fill them in gives students independence and confidence in their ability to function successfully in an English language environment. The value of these skills cannot be overstated!

- Copy the blank **Vocabulary** form on the flip side of your handout for students to write definitions and translations of important vocabulary, or have them write words to remember in the **Vocabulary** section of their notebooks.

- As an alternative, hand out the lesson ahead of time and have students look up vocabulary words in their dictionaries for prereading homework before you work with the lesson in class. Ask them to circle unfamiliar words that they cannot find in their dictionaries.

- Ask students which words they could not find in their dictionaries. List the words on the board. Ask volunteers to give the meanings of any words they can. Write the meaning of each word—a synonym, definition, or paraphrase—on the board and have students copy the list on the **Vocabulary** flip side of their handout or in the Vocabulary section of their notebooks.

- Read and explain small written segments at a time, giving everyone the opportunity to listen to your pronunciation of the words and to practice pronouncing the words themselves.

- When you have completed the entire piece of writing, ask students questions about what you have just read. Some **Read with the Class** activities include comprehension questions. Add your own questions until you are sure that students comprehend all the significant parts of the writing.

Write with the Class

OBJECTIVE: *To decide cooperatively what to write with the whole class and how to fill in a writing model together; to create a list or collection of information about all class members.*

- There are a variety of **Write with the Class** activities: listing class information (foods students eat every day, kinds of soup students like, abbreviations from ads), and writing for different reasons (class greetings, invitations, and messages).

- In addition, many of the **Write** activities (intended for individual student fill-in writing activities) suggest, *"With your class, add more choices."* As the class adds more choices, you may prefer to convert it to a **Write with the Class** activity and fill in the writing model as a whole class first; then have students write another model independently.

- The instructions for these activities will vary. Start by reading the instructions together. Make sure everyone in the class understands the task.

- Select a volunteer to write the list or the message on the board.

- Ask the students for information for the list or ideas for the messages. As with a **Class Brainstorm**, write all the information and ideas on the board.

- Have the class refine messages by choosing phrases that the whole class prefers and by correcting spelling and grammar until everyone is satisfied with the writing.

- Discuss questions included at the end of the activity.

- Have students copy the lists or messages in the Activities section of their notebooks on the flip side of their handout.

GROUP ACTIVITIES

Cross-Cultural Exchange

OBJECTIVE: *To discuss in groups the practices or issues that are handled differently in different cultures or countries; to increase awareness of cultural diversity and the variety of individual experiences and perceptions; to practice withholding judgment.*

- Some of the **Cross-Cultural Exchange** activities in *A WRITING BOOK* are written as whole class activities; others are written as group activities. The group **Cross-Cultural Exchanges** are for topics or situations about which many students may be expected to have had prior knowledge. Depending on the experience and prior knowledge of the students in your class, you may want to vary the format of a **Cross-Cultural Exchange** from group to whole-class discussions or vice versa.

- Read all the questions together. Tell students that each group must give as many answers as possible to every question, and that the answers should be based on their own personal experiences.

- Explain the objective of the activity. Remind the students that everyone has different experiences and that in this activity it is important to try to understand differences rather than to judge them.

- Divide the class into groups.

- Have each group appoint a recorder to write down all the students' answers to each question.

- While the groups are asking and answering questions, circulate, help as needed. Whenever possible, have students share stories or teach their groups something interesting about their own culture or their own personal experiences within a culture. If students are all from the same country, experiential differences can be extremely interesting and insightful! This validates students' backgrounds, fosters self-esteem, and is essential in building a student-centered humanistic classroom.

- At the end of the group activity, bring the class together. Have the group recorders report the results of the discussions to the class. Have group members repeat interesting stories or pieces of cultural information for the whole class.

- Help the class summarize and compare the cultural information gathered.

Group Brainstorm

OBJECTIVE: *To encourage students to think about topics beyond bounds of "right" or "wrong." To tap into their prior knowledge and share and compare information with a group and with the whole class.*

- Review the concept of "brainstorming." Remind students that the recorder will be listing the ideas quickly.

- Divide the class into groups.

- Have each group choose a recorder who will be responsible for writing down all the words or ideas.

- Instruct the groups to call out to the recorder words or ideas associated with the topic.

- Remind students to work quietly and not to comment or make judgments.

- When the lists are completed, have the recorders read the lists to their groups.

- Advise the groups to edit their lists for vocabulary, grammar, and spelling.

- Ask each recorder to read his/her group's list to the class; then transcribe the list on the board.

- Erase any items repeated on more than one list.

- When the class list is complete, have students read the list aloud, make any final corrections, and discuss any items that are particularly appropriate or inappropriate.

- Have students copy the class list in their notebooks or on the **List** flip side of their handout.

Group Survey

OBJECTIVE: *To encourage students to voice opinions and preferences, to compare their preferences in groups, and to check accuracy in recording answers.*

- Divide the class into the recommended groups.

- Model the questions; have students repeat; check pronunciation. If appropriate, add one more item. Be sure students understand all the vocabulary and the objective of the activity before beginning the survey.

- If the survey is presented with columns to check off, tell students to check their own answers in the appropriate columns.

- If there are only survey questions listed on the page, have students write their own responses on the page.

- Instruct students to ask everyone in their group all the questions. To vary the method, tell students to take turns asking the questions and recording the answers in their group.

- While the students are working together, copy the questions on the board.

- Tell the groups to check their answers and make sure they all have the same totals.

- Have each group select a reporter to report its results to the class. Have a student volunteer write the numbers on the board next to each question.

- When all groups have reported, have the class add up all the numbers on the board for each question to find the class totals.

- To check the accuracy of the totals, ask the whole class the questions again. Have students raise hands to show responses; count the raised hands; write the numbers on the board. See if the survey was accurate!

Print with a Group

OBJECTIVE: *To practice printing legibly in appropriate situations with a group.*

- These activities appear in *Unit 1: Handwriting* for practice printing legibly, and in later units where students need to fill in forms that typically require printing. **Print with a Group** activities generally ask a small group of students to collaborate on filling in personal information or to brainstorm words and print them together.

- Explain to students that there are many styles of printing, but their printing should always be clear and legible. Many forms require printing because the information must be filled in legibly!

- Divide the class into the recommended groups. Explain that everyone in the group must write in this activity.

- Have the whole class read the instructions for the activity aloud. Make sure all students understand all parts of the activity before any groups start to brainstorm or print. Write sample fill-in answers on the board as needed.

- While the groups are working, circulate, help as needed.

- When the writing task is completed, have each group report to the class or share their writing with another group.

- Discuss with the whole class any questions, problems, or interesting bits of information that students learned during the activities.

Read with a Group

OBJECTIVE: *To practice cooperative reading in small groups, including reading for comprehension as well as reading journals and plans aloud.*

- These activities include reading journal entries and personal plans to a group, comparing addresses and "for sale" ads, as well as studying checkbook receipt pages, "help wanted" ads, and Social Security cards. In each activity, students must work cooperatively to read and understand.

- Divide the class into the recommended groups of three or four. Make sure the students in each group are sitting close enough to one another to be able to hear easily, and far enough away from other groups to avoid distraction.

- Tell the groups to choose someone to read the activity instructions aloud to their group and to make sure that everyone in the group understands the instructions. If anyone doesn't understand, explain the confusing part to the whole class.

- Set a time limit for the activity of five to fifteen minutes, depending on the activity.

- While students are completing the activity, circulate, help as needed.

- When the task is complete, have each group either report to the class or share and compare their results with another group.

- Discuss with the whole class any questions, problems, or interesting bits of information that arise.

Write with a Group

OBJECTIVE: *To complete everyday writing tasks cooperatively with a small group; to write something for a group, then edit the writing cooperatively.*

- **Write with a Group** activities vary widely from simple tasks such as writing and comparing signatures and writing amounts of money to complex, difficult assignments such as writing a cover letter for a résumé and writing questions about a rental agreement. However, all of the tasks have one essential thing in common: they depend on cooperative group work.

- Divide the class into recommended groups of three or four.

- Tell each group to choose someone to read the activity instructions aloud to their group, and then to make sure that everyone in the group understands the instructions. If anyone doesn't understand, explain the confusing part to the whole class.

- Set a time limit for the activity of five to fifteen minutes, depending on the activity.

- While students are completing the activity, circulate, help as needed.

- When the task is completed, have each group report to the class or share and compare their results with another group.

- Discuss with the whole class any questions, problems, or interesting bits of information that arise.

PARTNER ACTIVITIES

Dialog Journal

OBJECTIVE: *To give students the opportunity to record personal experiences, feelings, and thoughts in writing; to read and respond to other students' personal writing; to expand and reinforce students' personally-useful vocabulary.*

- Explain the objectives of this task and encourage freedom of expression.

- Tell students they are going to write a journal entry, then give it to a partner who will read it and respond in writing. If students have not done this activity before, write a sample dialog response for them on the board as a guide.

- In some cases, students will need to fill in journals. In other cases, and to continue their dialogs, they will fill in a blank Journal form on the flip side of their papers or write in the Journal section of their notebooks.

- The original journal entries may be done either in class or as a homework assignment.

- Divide the class into pairs and have each pair exchange journal entries.

- Give the class a time limit of about 15 minutes. Depending on the class, you may find it helpful to require that students not talk at all during this activity.

- While students are completing the activity, circulate, help as needed.

- As they complete their dialog responses, have students exchange journals again, read their partners' responses, and write back to their partner again.

- Students should continue writing back and forth to their partner on the topic as long as time and interest remains.

Listen and Write

OBJECTIVE: *To improve pronunciation, listening, and spelling by giving and taking dictation with a partner.*

- There is one **Listen and Write** activity in *A WRITING BOOK* (on p.110). In it, students dictate amounts of money to a partner, then check their partner's dictation. If your class enjoys partner dictation, consider adding it as a follow-up activity for writing dates, journal entries, greeting cards, addresses, signs, telephone messages, recipes, directions, and ads, using the flip side **Listen and Write** on the back of their handout.

- Divide the class into pairs.

- Tell the students to write five amounts of money on a piece of paper; they should not let their partner see what they have written!

- Explain that each student must dictate the five amounts of money to a partner slowly and with clear pronunciation. Model the pronunciation of some amounts of money as examples.

- While students are completing the activity, circulate, help as needed.

- When the students have finished writing, have them check and correct their partner's dictation.

- Discuss as a class any problems that students may have experienced with the dictation, especially with pronunciation, listening, and spelling.

- For additional practice and reinforcement, dictate "problem" words or phrases again, and have students write them on the **Listen and Write** flip side of their handout.

- If the pronunciation and listening skill level of the students in your class makes a partner dictation difficult, this activity may be converted to a whole-class dictation.

Partner Interview

OBJECTIVE: *To give students practice in asking and answering or in listening to and writing about a partner's experiences, then reading a partner's responses to other students.*

- Practice the interview questions with the students. Model the questions; have students repeat; check pronunciation. Be sure everyone understands the questions and the vocabulary. Supply additional words as needed.

- Divide the class into pairs.

- Tell the students to write their partner's answers to the interview questions in the notebooks or on the **Partner Interview** flip side of their handout.

- This activity requires students to ask in the second person *(you)*, listen to the partner's responses in the first person *(I)*, then write the response in the third person *(he or she)*. This is a good time to review third person grammar changes needed for the activity. Demonstrate the necessary changes by asking a student the first interview question, listening to the student's answer, asking the class how to write the answer, and writing the answer on the board in the third person.

- Give a time limit for the interview—usually about ten minutes.

- While students are completing the activity, circulate, help as needed.

- When the interviews are completed or the time is up, have each pair join another pair and read aloud their partner's responses to the questions.

Print with a Partner

OBJECTIVE: *To practice printing legibly in appropriate situations with a partner.*

- These activities appear in *Unit 1: Handwriting* for practice printing legibly, and in later units where students need to make maps and signs, abbreviate state names, and print notices.

- Explain to students that there are many styles of printing, but that whatever style they use, their printing should always be clear and legible. Maps, signs, notices, and abbreviations of state names are generally printed because they must always be easy to read.

- Divide the class into pairs.

- Make sure all students understand how to complete the activity together before they start.

- While students are completing the activity, circulate, help as needed. Discuss with the whole class any questions that come up during the process.

- When the pairs are finished, have them share their printed pieces with another pair or with the class.

Read with a Partner

OBJECTIVE: *To practice reading for comprehension cooperatively with a partner.*

- These activities include reading and answering questions with a partner about information on an envelope, on a bulletin board, and on an employment application. In each activity, students must work cooperatively to read and understand.

- Divide the class into pairs.

- Read the instructions together. Make sure everyone understands.

- Tell the class that each pair must take turns reading aloud sentences from the activity, that they must answer the questions together, and that both must write their answers on the **Listen and Write** flip side of their handout.

- Set a time limit for the activity of five to fifteen minutes, depending on the activity.

- While students are completing the activity, circulate, help as needed.

- When the task is completed, have each pair report to the class or read and compare their answers with another pair.

- Discuss with the whole class any questions, problems, or interesting bits of information that arise.

Write with a Partner

OBJECTIVE: *To complete everyday writing tasks cooperatively with a partner; to write something for a partner, then respond to the partner's writing.*

- **Write with a Partner** activities vary widely, and include writing greetings, schedules, messages, dates, letters, lists, phone conversations, recipes, and directions. All of the tasks have one essential thing in common: they depend on writing cooperatively with a partner.

- Divide the class into pairs.

- Read the instructions together. Make sure all students understand how to complete the activity together before they start. If anyone doesn't understand, explain the confusing part to the whole class.

- Set a time limit of ten to twenty minutes, depending on the activity.

- While students are completing the activity, circulate, help as needed. Discuss with the whole class any questions, problems, or interesting bits of information that arise.

- When the task is completed, have each pair report to the class or read their writing to another pair of students.

INDIVIDUAL ACTIVITIES

Print

OBJECTIVE: *To become familiar with situations in which printing is appropriate; to practice printing personal information legibly in those situations.*

- These activities appear in *Unit 1: Handwriting* to provide practice in printing legibly. In later units students fill in forms that typically require printing.

- Explain to students that there are many styles of printing, but whatever style they use, their printing should always be clear and legible. Many forms require printing because the information must be filled in legibly!

- **Print** activities typically follow a **Read with the Class** activity in which students study the vocabulary, meaning, and information required on a form. Make sure all students understand all parts of each form before they start to fill it in.

- If the form remains very difficult for the students in your class, change the format of the activity to **Print with the Class** and have everyone fill in the form together.

- While students are filling in the form, circulate, help as needed. Discuss with the whole class any questions that come up during the process.

- When students have finished the printing activity, have them exchange papers with a partner and read their partner's paper. Alternatively, have them exchange papers in groups of three or four.

- Discuss with the whole class any questions, problems, or interesting bits of information that arise.

Write

OBJECTIVE: *To personalize writing models of journals, greeting cards, invitations, notes, letters, directions, checks, recipes, forms, and ads by filling in specific, individual information; to practice using the conventions of these everyday writing tasks.*

- **Write** activities are individual writing tasks. Some are the central writing task of a lesson and require students to fill in a model on the lesson page itself. Others are follow-up tasks in which students write more from their own experience or for their own needs.

- The instructions for these activities will vary. Start by reading the instructions together. Make sure everyone in the class understands the task.

- Many of the fill-in **Write** activities start: *"With your class, add more choices."* For these activities, select a student volunteer to write the additional choices on the board. Students should copy the added words on their sheets.

- As the class adds choices, you may prefer to convert it to a **Write with the Class** activity and fill in the writing model as a whole class first. Then have students write another model independently on a blank flip side of the lesson sheet.

- Set a time limit for writing. Time limits for these activities will depend entirely on how fast students in your class can write in English. Experiment with different time limits, and be prepared to give the whole class more time if necessary.

- There will always be students who finish early—tell them to check over their writing in the remaining time or to write more on the flip side of their paper. There will also be students who can never finish within any time limit; their difficulties will need to be handled individually.

- While the students are writing, circulate, help as needed.

- After the writing is completed, have students exchange their writing with a partner and read their partner's writing. Alternatively, have students exchange writing in groups of three or four.

- Discuss with the whole class any questions, problems, or interesting bits of information that arise.

A WRITING BOOK
English in Everyday Life
A Teacher's Resource Book
Second Edition

HANDWRITING

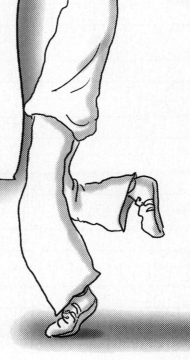

SPELLING HINT

➤ The **ch sound** is usually spelled **ch**. Sometimes it is spelled **tch**.

check	in**ch**	sti**tch**
children	pin**ch**	stre**tch**
chur**ch**	whi**ch**	ca**tch**

PRINT WITH UPPERCASE LETTERS

Cross-Cultural Exchange

Recite the English alphabet with your class. • Print it on the board. • Print alphabets for other languages on the board. • Recite them. • Compare the alphabets. • What is similar? • What is different?

Print

Print the English alphabet with uppercase (capital) letters. • Follow the arrows.

A A

B B

C C

D D

E E

F F

G G

H H

I I

J J

K K

L L

M M M

N N N

O O O

P P P

Q Q Q

R R R

S S S

T T T

U U U

V V V

W W W

X X X

Y Y Y

Z Z Z

PRINT WITH UPPERCASE LETTERS, p. 3

Print with a Group

In groups of four, print the names of all the students in your group. • Begin with your own name. • Use capital letters. • Who has the longest name in your group? • Who has the shortest name?

Your first name

Your last name

GROUP NAMES

First name

Last name

First name

Last name

First name

Last name

PRINT WITH LOWERCASE LETTERS

Print with a Partner

Use the lowercase alphabet below. • Trace all the letters of the alphabet that are in your name. • Follow the arrows. • Trace all the letters that are in your partner's names. • Then print the letters that are in your name and in your partner's name.

a   a

b   b

c   c

d   d

e   e

f   f

g   g

h   h

i   i

j   j

k   k

l

m m

n n

o o

p p

q q

r r

s s

t t

u u

v v

w w

x x

y y

z z

PRINT WITH LOWERCASE LETTERS, p. 3

Print with Your Class

Do you know other ways to print some of the lowercase letters in the English alphabet? •
Print them on the board. • Then copy them here.

_____

- -

_____

Print with a Group

In groups of four, print a word that begins with each letter of the alphabet. • Compare your
list with another group. • Then compare it with the whole class.

a _____   j _____   s _____

b _____   k _____   t _____

c _____   l _____   u _____

d _____   m _____   v _____

e _____   n _____   w _____

f _____   o _____   x _____

g _____   p _____   y _____

h _____   q _____   z _____

i _____   r _____

PRINT WITH UPPER AND LOWERCASE LETTERS

Print with a Group
Print the complete alphabet.

A a   N n

B b   O o

C c   P p

D d   Q q

E e   R r

F f   S s

G g   T t

H h   U u

I i   V v

J j   W w

K k   X x

L l   Y y

M m   Z z

PRINT WITH UPPER AND LOWERCASE LETTERS, p. 2

Print with a Group

In groups of four, print your whole name. • *Begin each name with an uppercase letter.* • *Use lowercase for all other letters in your name.*

_____
- -
_____

Show your name to the other students in your group. • *Say your name.* • *Say the names of the other students in your group.* • *Print their names with capital and small letters below.*

_____
- -
_____
- -
_____
- -
_____
- -
_____

Print with your Class

What letters of the alphabet are not in anyone's name in your class? • *Print the names of all the students in your class on the board.* • *Copy each name in your notebook.*

WRITE WITH UPPERCASE LETTERS

Class Discussion

Read this alphabet together. • Do you write capital (uppercase) letters this way? • Which capital letters do you write differently? • Write other styles of capital letters on the board. • What are the most common differences in your class?

Write

Write the English alphabet in capital letters. • Follow the arrows.

WRITE WITH LOWERCASE LETTERS

Write

Practice writing these lowercase letters. • *Follow the arrows.* • *Then copy each letter several times.*

Write with a Group

In groups of four, write a word that begins with each letter of the English alphabet. •
Compare your group's list with another group's list.

a	n
b	o
c	p
d	q
e	r
f	s
g	t
h	u
i	v
j	w
k	x
l	y
m	z

WRITE WITH LOWERCASE LETTERS, p. 4

Class Survey

Read the seven questions. • *With your class, add another question.* • *Put a* ✔ *under* WRITE *or* PRINT. • *Report your answers to the class.*

	WRITE	PRINT
1. Do you prefer to **write** or **print** a letter to someone?	_____	_____
2. Do you prefer to **write** or **print** your signature?	_____	_____
3. Do you prefer to **write** or **print** notes?	_____	_____
4. Do you prefer to **write** or **print** your homework?	_____	_____
5. Do you prefer to **write** or **print** shopping lists?	_____	_____
6. Do you prefer to **write** or **print** a sign?	_____	_____
7. Do you prefer to **write** or **print** a telephone message?	_____	_____
8. Other: _____	_____	_____

- How many students write most of the time? _____
- How many students print most of the time? _____

WRITE YOUR SIGNATURE

Class Discussion

With your class, compare the signatures of two famous Americans: John Hancock in the 1770's and John F. Kennedy in the 1960's. • Which is easier to read?

Write with a Group

In groups of four, write your signature. Then answer the questions below.

Signatures
1. _____
2. _____
3. _____
4. _____
5. _____

Class Survey

How many signatures are whole names? _____

How many are initials? _____

How many are difficult to read? _____

How many are easy to read? _____

Cross-Cultural Exchange

Write your whole name on the board in your language. • Read your name to the class. • Write your signature in your language if it is different from your whole name. • Is your signature the same in your native language and in English? • Is it more important for a signature to be easy to read or for a signature to be individual?

WRITE TIME ABBREVIATIONS

Read with the Class

In English, the abbreviations for time can be written different ways for "ante meridiem" (a.m., AM), the first twelve hours of the day, and "post meridiem" (p.m., PM), the last twelve hours of the day.

A.M. and **P.M.**   **AM** and **PM**   **a.m.** and **p.m.**

7:00 a.m.	seven o'clock in the morning
12:00 p.m.	twelve o'clock noon; midday
3:15 p.m.	three-fifteen in the afternoon
8:30 p.m.	eight-thirty in the evening
12:00 a.m.	twelve o'clock at night; midnight

Write

Write the numbers and abbreviations for the times below. • *Include one of the following in each answer: A.M., AM, a.m., P.M., PM, p.m.* • *Check your answers with the class.*

1. two forty-five in the afternoon _____

2. five after twelve, midday _____

3. twenty past nine in the morning _____

4. two-fifty in the middle of the night _____

5. five to eight in the evening _____

Partner Interview   Partner's Name _____

Discuss these questions with your partner. • *Then write numbers and time abbreviations.*

1. What time does this class end? _____

2. What time does a new year begin? _____

3. What time did you get up this morning? *You:* _____

   Partner: _____

4. What time did you get up last Sunday? *You:* _____

   Partner: _____

WRITE DATES

Read with the Class

Abbreviations for Months

January	Jan.	July	*
February	Feb.	August	Aug.
March	Mar.	September	Sept.
April	Apr.	October	Oct.
May	*	November	Nov.
June	*	December	Dec.

* Note: May, June, and July are not usually abbreviated.

Write

Study the three ways that the first date is written. • *Then fill in the other two ways to show each date.*

January 22, 1996	**Jan. 22, 1996**	**1/22/96**
February 14, 2000	_____	_____
_____	Dec. 25, 1940	_____
_____	_____	3/7/64
_____	Aug. 18, 1932	_____
September 3, 2001	_____	_____
_____	_____	10/2/00
_____	_____	4/11/97
November 4, 2003	_____	_____

Write with a Partner

Partner's Name _____

Write these dates three ways with a partner.

1. Today's date: _____ _____ _____

2. Your birthdate: _____ _____ _____

3. Your partner's birthdate: _____ _____ _____

4. The first day of this class: _____ _____ _____

5. The last date of this class: _____ _____ _____

UNIT 2

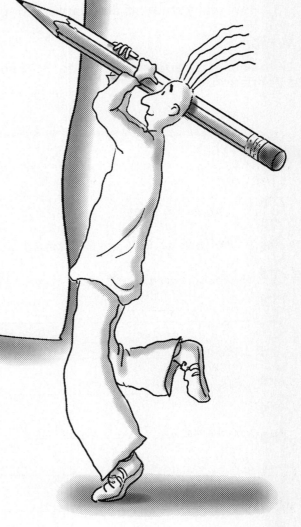

JOURNALS

SPELLING HINT

➤ The **k sound** is usually spelled **c, k, ck,** or **ch**.

cash	**k**eep	qui**ck**ly	stoma**ch**
pi**c**ni**c**	**k**ing	o'**c**lo**ck**	a**ch**e
a**c**tive	loo**k**	tru**ck**	**ch**orus

JOURNAL: PERSONAL INFORMATION

Class Survey

Survey your class. • Ask these questions. • Write the results on the board.

1. What countries are the students from?
2. What languages do the students speak?
3. How many students are married? single?
4. How many students have children?
5. How many students live with their family?

Write

With your class, add more choices. • Then fill in the journal entry with your personal information.

_____ (1)

Today I am going to write about myself. I am from _____ (2), and I speak _____ (3). I was born on _____ (4). I am _____ (5) years old. I am _____ (6), and I have _____ (7). I live _____ (8) in _____ (9).

1. Today's date
2. Your native country
3. The languages you speak
4. Your date of birth
5. Your age
6. Choose one:
   * *single*
   * *married*
   * *divorced*
   * *separated*
   * *widowed*
7. Choose one:
   * *no children*
   * *one child*
   * *two children*
   * *other:*

   _____

8. Choose one:
   * *by myself*
   * *with my family*
   * *with relatives*
   * *other:*

   _____

9. City/town, and state/country

Dialog Journal

Partner's Name _____

Read a partner's journal entry. • Write a response to your partner's journal entry. • Combine with another pair. • Read your journal entry to the group. • Discuss all the entries.

JOURNAL: MY FAMILY

Partner Interview

Partner's Name _____

Ask your teacher these questions. • *Then ask a partner.* • *Write your partner's answers in your notebook.*

1. What is today's date?
2. How many people are in your family?
3. How many brothers and sisters do you have?
4. What are their names?

5. What are your parents' names?
6. How many children do you have?
7. What are their names?

Write

With your class, add more choices. • *Then fill in the journal entry about your family.*

_____ (1)

There are _____ (2) *people in my family. I have* _____ (3) *brother(s) and* _____ (3) *sister(s). Their names are* _____ (4) *and* _____ (4). *My parents names are* _____ (5) *and* _____ (5). *I have* _____ (6) *children. Their names are* _____ (7) *and* _____ (7).

1. Today's date
2. Choose one:
   • *two*
   • *three*
   • *four*
   • other:

   _____

3. Choose one:
   • *no*
   • *one*
   • *two*
   • other:

   _____

4. (Names of brothers and sisters)
5. Names of parents
6. Choose one:
   • *no*
   • *two*
   • *three*
   • other:

   _____

7. Names of children

Dialog Journal

Partner's Name _____

Read a partner's journal entry. • *Write a response to your partner's journal entry.*

Read to the Class

Bring in a family photo. • *Read your paragraph to the class and show your photo.*

JOURNAL: TODAY

Write with a Group

In groups of three, make a list of things you all do every day. • Compare lists with another group.

Write

With your class, add more choices. • Then fill in the journal entry about today.

1. Day of the week
2. Today's date
3. Choose one:
   • *happy*
   • *homesick*
   • *tired*
   • *nervous*
   • other:
   _____

4. Choose one:
   • *working*
   • *studying*
   • *shopping*
   • *other:*
   _____

5. Choose one:
   • *eat*
   • *do my homework*
   • *go to bed*
   • *other:*

Read with a Group

In groups of four, read your journal entries. • Discuss the entries. • Decide which one to read to the class.

Write with a Partner   Partner's Name _____

Make a schedule of all the things you have to do this week. • Exchange schedules with a partner • Read and compare your schedules.

Write

In the Journal section of your notebook, write a journal entry about your favorite day of the week. • Explain why it is your favorite day.

Read to the Class

Read your journal entry to the class. • Then discuss reasons for favorite days with your classmates.

JOURNAL: IN THE MORNING

Partner Interview
Partner's Name _____

Ask your teacher these questions. • *Then ask a partner.* • *Write your partner's answers in the Activities section of your notebook.*

1. What is today's date?
2. What time do you get up every day?
3. What do you usually have for breakfast?
4. How do you feel every morning?

Write

With your class, add more choices. • *Then fill in the journal entry about your morning.*

_____ (1)

I usually get up at _____ (2).
I _____ (3) *and*
_____ (3). *I have*
_____ (4) *for*
breakfast. I usually feel
_____ (5) *in the*
morning. Today I feel _____ (6)
_____.

1. Today's date
2. Time you get up
3. Choose two:
   • *get dressed*
   • *take a shower*
   • *comb my hair*
   • other:

   _____

4. Choose one or more:
   • *nothing*
   • *a cup of coffee*
   • *a piece of toast*
   • other:

   _____

5. Choose one or more:
   • *energetic*
   • *sleepy*
   • *grouchy*
   • other:

   _____

6. Choose one or more:
   • *wonderful*
   • *tired*
   • *sick*
   • other:

   _____

Read with a Group

In groups of four, read your journal entries. • *Discuss the entries. Decide which one to read to the class.*

Write with a Partner
Partner's Name _____

Make a list of the things you have to do today. • *Read a partner's list.* • *Compare your lists.* • *Who has more things to do today?*

JOURNAL: WEATHER

Partner Interview

Partner's Name _____

Ask your teacher these questions. • *Then ask a partner.* • *Write your partner's answers in the Activities section of your notebook.*

1. What are some words that describe the weather today?
2. How do you feel today?
3. What do you want to do today?

Write

With your class, add more choices. • *Then fill in the journal entry about the weather today.*

_____ (1)

Today is a _____ (2)

day. It is very _____ (3).

It is a good day to _____ (4)

_____

and _____ (4)

_____.

1. Today's date
2. Choose one:
   • *rainy*
   • *cloudy*
   • *sunny*
   • other:

   _____

3. Choose one:
   • *hot*
   • *cold*
   • *cool*
   • *other:*

   _____

4. Choose one or more:
   • *go to the movies*
   • *study English*
   • *sleep*
   • *other:*

   _____

Read with a Group

In groups of four, read your journal entries. • *Discuss the entries.* • *Decide which one to read to the class.*

Write

Every day for one week, write a journal entry about the weather in the Journal section of your notebook.

Cross-Cultural Exchange

What's the weather like today in your country? In other parts of the world? • *Tell the class.* • *Write a class list of the weather in different places.*

JOURNAL: FAVORITE HOLIDAY

Write with the Class

List everyone's favorite holiday on the board.

Partner Interview

Partner's Name _____

Ask your teacher these questions. • Then ask a partner. • Write your partner's answers in your notebook.

1. What is today's date?
2. What is your favorite holiday?
3. What is the date of your favorite holiday?
4. What's the weather like on that day?

5. What do you do on that day?
6. What special food do you eat?
7. Why do you like this holiday best?

Write

With your class, add more choices. • Then fill in the journal entry about your favorite holiday.

_____ (1)

My favorite holiday is _____ (2) _____. The date is _____ (3) _____. The weather is usually _____ (4) _____. On that day, I usually _____ (5) _____. A typical food for the holiday is _____ (6) _____. I like this holiday because _____ (7) _____.

1. Today's date
2. Choose one:
   - *Christmas*
   - *New Year's Day*
   - other:

   _____

3. Date of your holiday
4. Choose one:
   - *cold*
   - *warm*
   - other:

   _____

5. Choose one:
   - *go to church*
   - *visit my family*
   - other:

   _____

6. Choose one:
   - *turkey*
   - *ham*
   - other:

   _____

7. Choose one:
   - *the parades are fun*
   - *my family is together*
   - other:

   _____

JOURNAL: THINKING ABOUT LIFE

Class Brainstorm

What kind of person are you? • *What do you like? What don't you like?* • *Write lists on the board.* • *Use these three headings:* **KINDS OF PEOPLE**   **LIKE**   **DON'T LIKE.**

Write

With your class, add more choices. • *Then fill in the journal entry about yourself.* • *Don't write your name.*

_____ (1)

    I have been thinking about myself today. I think I am basically a _____ (2) person. I enjoy _____ (3) _____ very much, and I love _____ (4) _____ .

One thing I don't like to do is _____ (5) .

1. Today's date
2. Choose one:
   • *practical*
   • *fun-loving*
   • *quiet*
   • *other:*
   _____

3. Choose one:
   • *being alone*
   • *being with people*
   • *studying*
   • *other:*
   _____

4. Choose one:
   • *to travel*
   • *to watch TV*
   • *to go out with friends*
   • *other:*
   _____

5. Choose one:
   • *be alone*
   • *go to parties*
   • *get up early*
   • *other:*
   _____

Class Game: Guess Who?

Fold your journal entries. • *Put them in a pile.* • *Choose one and read it to the class.* • *Guess who wrote the journal.*

Write with a Group

Write a paragraph about something you like to do or you don't like to do. • *In groups of three or four, read your paragraphs.* • *Who likes or dislikes the same things?*

JOURNAL: BELIEFS AND OPINIONS

Class Survey

Add to this list. • *Then survey your class.* • *Write the results on the board.* • *How many students in the class have strong beliefs or opinions about each topic listed?*

1. religion
2. politics
3. marriage
4. family life
5. women's issues
6. other: _____

Write

With your class, add more choices. • *Then fill in the entry about your beliefs and opinions.*

_____ (1)

I have strong opinions about _____ (2). I _____ (3) talk about my beliefs, because most of the people around me _____ (4).

1. Today's date
2. Choose one:
   • *politics*
   • *religion*
   • *marriage*
   • *family life*
   • *women's issues*
   • *other:*
   _____
3. Choose one:
   • *often*
   • *rarely*
   • *never*
   • *other:*
   _____
4. Choose one:
   • *agree with me*
   • *don't agree with me*
   • *are interested*
   • *aren't interested*
   • *other:*
   _____

Dialog Journal

Partner's Name _____

Read a partner's journal entry. • *Write a response to your partner.*

Write with a Group

Write a paragraph in the Activities section of your notebook about one of your beliefs and opinions. • *In groups of three or four read and discuss your paragraphs.* • *Who in your group has the same opinions or beliefs?*

JOURNAL: A DAY AT WORK

Partner Interview

Partner's Name _____

Ask your teacher these questions • Then ask a partner. • Write your partner's answers in your notebook.

1. What time did you begin work yesterday?
2. What did you do at work?
3. What did you do first?
4. What time did you end your workday?
5. Was it a good day or a bad day at work? Why?

Write

With your class, add more choices. • Then fill in the journal entry about a day at work.

_____ (1)

_____ (2) I had a

_____ (3) _____ (4)

at work. I work for _____ (5)

_____ as a(n)

_____ (6) .

I started work at _____ (7)

and finished at _____ (8) . I

_____ (9)

_____ . It was a

very _____ (10) day.

1. The date
2. Choose one:
   • *Last Monday*
   • *Tuesday*
   • other:

   _____

3. Choose one:
   • *bad*
   • *great*
   • other:

   _____

4. Choose one:
   • *day*
   • *evening*
   • *afternoon*
   • other:

   _____

5. Name of the place you work
6. Title of your job
7. Time you started work today
8. Time you ended work today
9. Choose one:
   • *had an easy time*
   • *worked very hard*
   • other:

   _____

10. Choose one:
    • *ordinary*
    • *unusual*
    • other:

    _____

28

GREETINGS

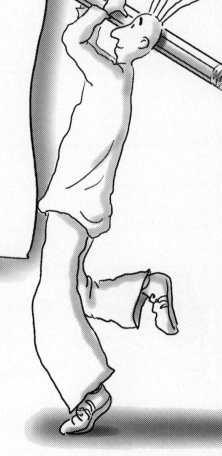

SPELLING HINT

➤ To form the plural of short words that end in **s**, **ss**, **sh**, **ch**, **tch**, **x**, or **zz**, add **es**. To form the plural of most other words, just add **s**.

ga**s**/gas**es**	lun**ch**/lunch**es**	bu**zz**/buzz**es**
dre**ss**/dress**es**	wa**tch**/watch**es**	word/word**s**
di**sh**/dish**es**	bo**x**/box**es**	car/car**s**

BIRTHDAY CARDS

Class Survey

Survey your class. • *Write the results on the board.*

- Who has a birthday this month?
- Who will have a birthday next month?
- Who had a birthday last month?
- How many students have a birthday in January? in February? etc.
- Which month has the most students' birthdays?

Write with a Partner   Partner's Name _____

With your class, add more choices. • *Then write a birthday card greeting for your partner.* • *Give it to your partner.*

Dear _____,
_____(1)

_____(2)

_____(3)

_____.

_____(4),

_____(5)

1. Your partner's birthday
2. Your partner's name
3. Choose one:
   - *Wishing you a wonderful birthday!*
   - *Have a happy day!*
   - *Best wishes today and always!*
   - other:

   _____

4. Choose one:
   - *Sincerely*
   - *Love*
   - *Fondly*
   - other:

   _____

5. Your signature

Cross-Cultural Exchange

How do you write "Happy Birthday" in your language? • *Write it on the board.* • *Teach the class the pronunciation.*

Community Activity

Which stores in your community sell birthday cards? • *Write the names of the stores on the board.* • *Visit one store and look at the birthday cards.* • *Do you understand the words?* • *Copy any words or phrases you don't understand. Discuss them with your class.*

VALENTINES

Partner Interview

Partner's Name _____

Ask your teacher these questions. • Then ask a partner. • Write your partner's answers in your notebook.

1. Do you celebrate Valentine's Day?
2. To whom do you give cards or presents on Valentine's Day? What do you give?
3. Do you ever receive cards or presents on Valentine's Day? What do you receive?
4. What are other good valentine gifts?

Write

With your class, add more choices. • Then write this valentine to someone you love.

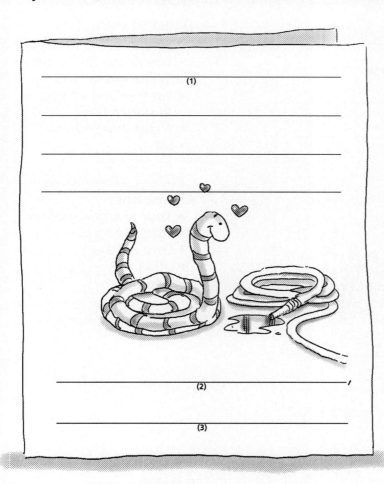

1. Copy this valentine verse:
   Roses are red,
   Violets are blue,
   Sugar is sweet,
   And so are you.

2. Choose one:
   - *Love*
   - *All my love*
   - *Yours forever*
   - *other:*

   _____

3. Choose one:
   - *Your Secret Admirer*
   - *Guess Who?*
   - *(your signature)*

Write with the Class

Make up a new valentine verse with your class. • Write it on the board. • Copy it in your notebook.

Write

Create a real valentine card. • Give it to someone you love.

MOTHER'S DAY CARDS

Partner Interview

Partner's Name _____

Ask your teacher these questions. • *Then ask a partner.* • *Write your partner's answers in your notebook.*

1. What is your mother's name?
2. How many sons and daughters does she have?
3. Where does she live?
4. How often do you see her?
5. What do you do on Mother's Day?

Write

With your class, add more choices. • *Then write a greeting on this Mother's Day card.*

(1)

(2)

(3)

(4)

1. Date this year
2. Choose one:
   - *You're the best mother in the world!*
   - *I'm thinking of you on Mother's Day*
   - *Thanks, Mom!*
   - other:

   _____

3. Choose one:
   - *Your loving daughter*
   - *Your loving son*
   - *Love always*
   - other:

   _____

4. Sign your first name.

Cross-Cultural Exchange

Answer these questions with your class. • *Write the answers on the board.*

Do people celebrate Mother's Day in your country? • *How do they celebrate?* • *In the United States, Mother's Day is the third Sunday in May.* • *Is it the same day in your country?* • *Who is a mother in our class?*

Write with the Class

In the United States, the third Sunday in June is Father's Day. • *Is it the same day in your country?* • *Who is a father in our class?* • *Write messages for Father's Day on the board.*

CONGRATULATIONS!

Class Brainstorm

Make a list on the board of reasons to say "Congratulations!"

Write

With your class, add more choices. • *Then write congratulations to a friend.*

Dear _____,
(1)

Congratulations on _____
(2)

_____.

_____
(3)

_____,
(4)

_____
(5)

1. A friend's name
2. Choose one:
   • *your new home*
   • *your new job*
   • *your new baby*
   • other:

   _____

3. Choose one:
   • *I'm so happy for you*
   • *How wonderful!*
   • other:

   _____

4. Choose one:
   • *Love*
   • *As ever*
   • other:

   _____

5. Your name

Write With a Partner   Partner's Name _____

Ask your partner: "What good thing has happened in your life recently?" • *Write a message to congratulate your partner.*

Read to the Class

Read your congratulations card to the class. • *Tell the class about the good event in your partner's life.*

THINKING OF YOU

Class Brainstorm

Read the messages for the card below. • *Make a list on the board of reasons to send a "Thinking of You" card.*

Write

With your class, add more choices. • *Then write a message to a friend or relative on this card.*

1. The name of a friend or relative
2. Choose one:
   - *I'm thinking of you today*
   - *My thoughts are with you*
   - *I wish I could be there with you*
   - other:

   _____

3. Choose one:
   - *I hope things are going well*
   - *I hope things are getting better*
   - *I hope we can get together soon*
   - other:

   _____

4. Choose one:
   - *Love*
   - *Always*
   - other:

   _____

5. Your first name

Write

Make a "Thinking of You" card for a friend or relative. • *Write a message on the card.* • *Give it to your friend or relative.*

GET-WELL CARDS

Class Brainstorm

Is any classmate sick and not in school today? • What could you write on a card? • Make a list on the board of things you can say in a card to a sick friend.

Write with a Partner

With your class, add more choices. • Write a get-well message to your partner on this card.

Dear _____ ,
(1)

_____
(2)

_____ .

_____
(3)

_____ .

_____ ,
(4)

_____
(5)

1. Your partner's name
2. Choose one:
   • *I'm sorry you're not feeling well*
   • *I'm sorry to hear about your accident*
   • other:

   _____

3. Choose one:
   • *I hope you'll be better soon*
   • *Wishing you a speedy recovery*
   • other:

   _____

4. Choose one:
   • *Love*
   • *Sincerely*
   • other:

   _____

5. Your signature

Community Activity

Look at the get-well cards in a store in your community. • What do they say? • Buy or make a get-well card and bring it to class. • Show your card to the class.

Write with the Class

Is anyone in your class really sick or injured? • If so, send a get-well card from the class.

SYMPATHY CARDS

Cross-Cultural Exchange

Answer these questions with your class. • *Write the answers on the board.*

1. In your culture, do people send sympathy cards when someone has died? What do the cards look like?
2. When someone has died, how do you express sympathy in your language? What do you say?

Write

With your class, add more choices. • *Then fill in this sympathy card.*

In Sympathy

(1)

(2)

(3)

1. Choose one:
   - *In this time of sadness, my prayers are with you.*
   - *I was so sorry to hear of your loss.*
   - *My thoughts are with you.*
   - other:

   _____

2. Choose one:
   - *Sincerely*
   - *Truly yours*
   - *With all my sympathy*
   - *Love*
   - other:

   _____

3. Your signature

Cross-Cultural Exchange

What do friends and relatives do in your home country when a person dies?

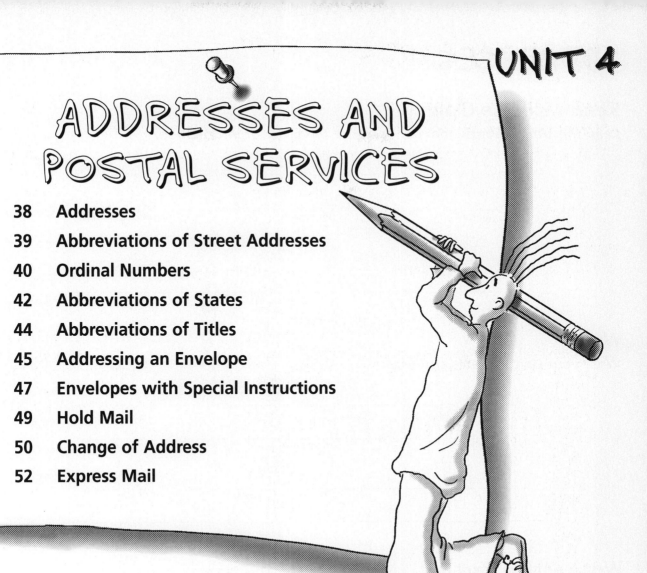

UNIT 4

ADDRESSES AND POSTAL SERVICES

SPELLING HINTS

➤ When a word ends in silent **e,** drop the **e** before adding **ing.**

giv**e**/giv**ing**	tak**e**/tak**ing**	writ**e**/writ**ing**
danc**e**/danc**ing**	invit**e**/invit**ing**	believ**e**/believ**ing**
hav**e**/hav**ing**	mak**e**/mak**ing**	lov**e**/lov**ing**

ADDRESSES

Read with the Class

Read this United States address. • *Notice the order of information.*

350	*Washington Street*	*Apt. 12*
(number)	(street name)	(apartment number)
New York	*New York*	*10001*
(city)	(state)	(ZIP code)

Write

Write your United States address.

(number)	(street name)	(apartment number)
(city)	(state)	(ZIP code)

Write with a Partner   Partner's Name _____

Write your partner's address.

(number)	(street name)	(apartment number)
(city)	(state)	(ZIP code)

Cross-Cultural Exchange

On the board, write addresses from different countries. • *Compare the different ways to write addresses.* • *The abbreviation for the United States of America is US, U.S., or U.S.A.* • *Is there an abbreviation in English for your country?* • *Write it on the board.*

ABBREVIATIONS OF STREET ADDRESSES

Write with a Group

In groups of three or four, copy the correct abbreviation next to each of the words below. •
Check your answers with the class.

St	Rd	Ct	Blvd	Ave or Av
Sq	Ln	Pk	Cir	Dr

1. Avenue _____

2. Boulevard _____

3. Circle _____

4. Court _____

5. Drive _____

6. Lane _____

7. Park _____

8. Road _____

9. Square _____

10. Street _____

Write with a Group

Copy the correct abbreviation next to each of the words below. • Check your answers with
the class.

N	RFD	W	PO	Apt	SW
SE		E	NW	S	NE

1. Apartment _____

2. Post Office _____

3. Rural Free Delivery _____

4. North _____

5. South _____

6. East _____

7. West _____

8. Northeast _____

9. Northwest _____

10. Southeast _____

11. Southwest _____

Write

Write your street address _underline_ *without* abbreviations.

_____

Write your street address _underline_ *with* abbreviations.

_____

Read with a Group

In groups of three or four, compare your addresses. • Are your abbreviations the same? • Are
they different? • Are they all correct? • If not, correct them in your group.

ORDINAL NUMBERS

Read with the Class

Look at the Ordinal Number Chart below. • Do any streets where you live have ordinal number names? (Example: Fifth Street) • Read the chart together.

Ordinal Number Chart

1st	first	20th	twentieth
2nd	second	21st	twenty-first
3rd	third	22nd	twenty-second
4th	fourth	23rd	twenty-third
5th	fifth	24th	twenty-fourth
6th	sixth	25th	twenty-fifth
7th	seventh	26th	twenty-sixth
8th	eighth	27th	twenty-seventh
9th	ninth	28th	twenty-eighth
10th	tenth	29th	twenty-ninth
11th	eleventh	30th	thirtieth
12th	twelfth	40th	fortieth
13th	thirteenth	50th	fiftieth
14th	fourteenth	60th	sixtieth
15th	fifteenth	70th	seventieth
16th	sixteenth	80th	eightieth
17th	seventeenth	90th	ninetieth
18th	eighteenth	100th	one hundredth
19th	nineteenth	200th	two hundredth

Listen and Write

Listen to your teacher read different ordinal numbers from the list. • Write each ordinal number two ways.

_____   _____   _____   _____

_____   _____   _____   _____

_____   _____   _____   _____

_____   _____   _____   _____

_____   _____   _____   _____

ORDINAL NUMBERS, p. 2

Write

*Write these street names as numbers. Use **St** for street and **Ave** for Avenue.*

Twenty-first Street   _____

Eighth Avenue   _____

Fifty-second Street   _____

Second Avenue   _____

Seventy-third Street   _____

Write

*Write these street names as words. This time, do not abbreviate **Street** or **Avenue**.*

12th Ave   _____

9th St   _____

58th St   _____

45th Ave   _____

121st St   _____

Community Activity

On your way home from class today, look for streets with ordinal number names. • Are they written with numbers or words? • Copy the street names. • Tell the class about them. • List them on the board. • Copy them in the Vocabulary section of your notebook.

Bring maps or telephone directories of different communities to class. • Find street addresses with ordinal number names. • How are they written? • List them on the board. • Copy them in the Vocabulary section of your notebook.

ABBREVIATIONS OF STATES

Read with the Class

Read the names and abbreviations of the fifty states along with the District of Columbia in the United States. • *Then practice writing the names of the states and their abbreviations in the Activities section of your notebook.*

Alabama (AL)	Idaho (ID)	Missouri (MO)	Pennsylvania (PA)
Alaska (AK)	Illinois (IL)	Montana (MT)	Rhode Island (RI)
Arizona (AZ)	Indiana (IN)	Nebraska (NB)	South Carolina (SC)
Arkansas (AR)	Iowa (IA)	Nevada (NV)	South Dakota (SD)
California (CA)	Kansas (KS)	New Hampshire (NH)	Tennessee (TN)
Colorado (CO)	Kentucky (KY)	New Jersey (NJ)	Texas (TX)
Connecticut (CT)	Louisiana (LA)	New Mexico (NM)	Utah (UT)
Delaware (DE)	Maine (ME)	New York (NY)	Vermont (VT)
District of Columbia (DC)	Maryland (MD)	North Carolina (NC)	Virginia (VA)
	Massachusetts (MA)	North Dakota (ND)	Washington (WA)
Florida (FL)	Michigan (MI)	Ohio (OH)	West Virginia (WV)
Georgia (GA)	Minnesota (MN)	Oklahoma (OK)	Wisconsin (WI)
Hawaii (HI)	Mississippi (MS)	Oregon (OR)	Wyoming (WY)

Listen and Write

Listen to your teacher say the names of fifteen states from the list. • *Write the name and the abbreviation of each state. (Example: Alaska AK)*

1. _____
2. _____
3. _____
4. _____
5. _____
6. _____
7. _____
8. _____

9. _____
10. _____
11. _____
12. _____
13. _____
14. _____
15. _____

ABBREVIATIONS OF STATES, p. 2

Print with a Partner

Partner's Name _____

Print the correct abbreviation for each state on this map of the United States.

Class Brainstorm

Make a list on the board of abbreviations for names of countries.

Cross-Cultural Exchange

In groups of four, write the names of states, regions, or provinces in your countries (if your home countries have states, regions, or provinces). • If you wish, choose one of these countries and write about it: Canada, Mexico, Brazil, France, Russia, Japan. • Then write the abbreviation for each.

ABBREVIATIONS OF TITLES

Read with the Class

Read these abbreviations with your class. Abbreviations are short forms of words.
(Example: Dr. = doctor)

Ms.	Miss	Jr.	Dr.	Dir.	Sen.	Pres.	Rev.
Mrs.	Mr.	Sr.	Prof.	Gov.	Rep.	Hon.	

Write with a Group

In groups of three or four, match these abbreviations of titles with the appropriate words. •
Compare your answers with the class.

Title   **Explanation**

_____   1. any man

_____   2. a married woman

_____   3. the leader of an association or a country

_____   4. a son with the same name as his father

_____   5. a professor

_____   6. any woman

_____   7. an unmarried woman or young girl

_____   8. an elected representative in the government

_____   9. a father with the same name as his son

_____   10. a doctor or dentist

_____   11. a governor of a state

_____   12. a director

_____   13. a senator in the government

_____   14. a judge in a court of law

_____   15. a priest or minister

Cross-Cultural Exchange

What are the equivalent titles for people in your country? • Do they have abbreviations? • If so,
write them on the board in your first language. • Then compare them with the titles on this page.

Group Brainstorm

Make a list of names of companies and government agencies with acronyms formed from their
first letters or syllables of the names. • Example: ZIP Code for Zone Improvement Plan Code •
Include both the acronym and the complete title. • Write your list on the board. • Compare it
with other groups' lists.

ADDRESSING AN ENVELOPE

Read with a Partner

Partner's Name _____

Look at the envelope below and answer these questions.

1. Who should it be sent to? _____

2. What is the street address? _____

3. What is the apartment number? _____

4. What town or city does the person live in? _____

5. What state does the person live in? _____

6. What is the ZIP Code? _____

7. Who is sending this? _____

8. What is the sender's complete return address? _____

_____

9. What date was this envelope postmarked? _____

P.T. Gomez
32 Lakeview Rd.
Newton, MA 02158

JUL 19
2000

Dr. William Rutledge
1508 Summit Ave. Apt. 6E
Hilldale, MA 01824

ADDRESSING AN ENVELOPE, p. 2

Write with a Partner

Partner's Name _____

Write the return address and the address on this envelope.

Return Address

1. Your name
2. Your street address or post office box number
3. Your city or town
4. Your state and Zip code

Address

5. Your partner's name
6. Your partner's street address or post office box number
7. Your partner's city or town
8. Your partner's state and Zip code

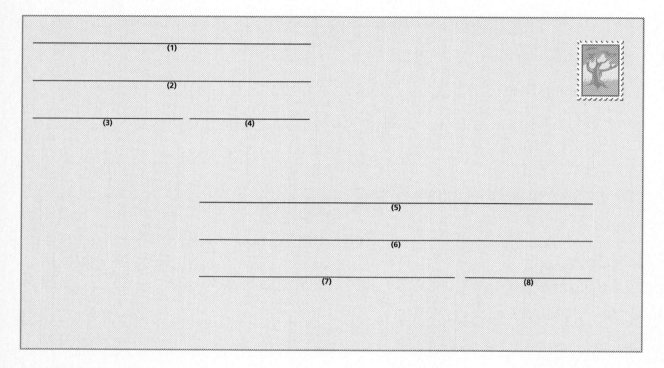

Write

Write a real letter to the same partner. • Put it in an envelope and address the envelope to your partner. • Include your return address.

Class Mail

Put all the letters in a class "mailbox." • Appoint one student to deliver the mail. • Read the letter from your partner.

Write with a Partner

Write a letter back to the same partner. • Put your letter in an envelope, address the envelope, put a stamp on it, and put it in a real mailbox.

ENVELOPES WITH SPECIAL INSTRUCTIONS

Read with a Partner

Partner's Name _____

Study this envelope with special instructions. • Then answer the questions below. • Compare your answers with the class.

R. Jones
26 Maple Rd
Fargo, SD   57701

Mr. John Doty
c/o Tito Lopez
1235 North Shore Drive
Raleigh, MI   27615

DISK ENCLOSED--DO NOT BEND!

1. Who is sending this? _____

2. What street does the sender live on? _____

3. What city does the sender live in? _____

   What state? _____

4. To whom is this envelope addressed? _____

5. With whom is he living? _____

6. What is in the envelope? _____

ENVELOPES WITH SPECIAL INSTRUCTIONS, p. 2

Write with a Partner

Partner's Name _____

*Imagine that you want to send a photo to your partner, who is visiting a friend. • Ask your partner for the friend's address. • Address this envelope to your partner, in care of the friend. • Include your return address. • Near the bottom of the envelope, write or print **Photo Enclosed.***

Write

Answer these questions about your envelope.

1. Who is the sender? _____

2. What is the sender's mailing address? _____

   _____

3. To whom is this envelope addressed? _____

4. What does c/o mean? _____

5. What is in the envelope? _____

HOLD MAIL

Read with the Class

*Refer to the **Authorization to Hold Mail** form to answer these questions.*

1. For how many days will the post office hold mail?
2. Will the post office deliver all your mail when you return?
3. What can you do if you don't know your return date?

UNITED STATES POSTAL SERVICE ™

Authorization to Hold Mail

This service has a 30 - day limit. See DMM 153.19.

Postmaster - Please hold mail for:

Name(s)

Address

Begin Holding Mail (Date)	Resume Delivery (Date)

A. I will pick up all accumulated mail when I return and understand that mail delivery will not resume until I do. (This is suggested if ☐ your return date may change or if no one will be at home to receive mail.)

B. Please deliver all accumulated mail and resume normal delivery ☐ on the ending date shown above.

Customer Signature

For Post Office Use Only

Date Received

Clerk	Bin Number
Carrier	Route Number

Customer Option A Only

Carrier: Accumulated mail has been picked up.   Resume delivery on:

_____   By: _____

PS Form **8076**   GPO : 1991 0 - 292-992

Class Survey

Survey your class. • Ask these questions. • Write the results on the board.

1. How many students ever go away for more than a few days?
2. How many students ask the post office to hold mail while they are away?
3. How many students knew about this service?

Write with a Partner   Partner's Name _____

Pretend you will take a trip. • Tell your partner about the trip you will take. • Fill in the ***Authorization to Hold Mail*** *form for the time you will be away.*

CHANGE OF ADDRESS

Read with the Class

*Read this sample **Change of Address Order**.*

U.S. Postal Service **CHANGE OF ADDRESS ORDER**	Instructions: Complete Items 1 thru 10. You must SIGN Item 9. Please PRINT all other items including address on face of card.	**OFFICIAL USE ONLY** Zone/Route ID No.

1. Change of Address for: *(Check one)*
   ☐ Individual ☒ Entire Family ☐ Business

2. Start Date: Month 06 Day 01 Year 00

3. Is This Move Temporary? *(Check one)*
   ☒ No ☐ Yes, Fill in ▶

4. If TEMPORARY move, print date to discontinue forwarding: Month Day Year

Date Entered on Form 3982 M M D D Y Y

Expiration Date M M D D Y Y

Clerk/Carrier Endorsement

5. Print Last Name (include Jr., Sr., etc.) or Name of Business (If more than one, use separate form for each).
   Lee

6. Print First Name (or Initial) and Middle Name (or Initial). Leave blank if for a business.
   John T.

7a. For Puerto Rico Only: If OLD mailing address is in Puerto Rico, print urbanization name, if appropriate.

7b. Print OLD mailing address: House/Building Number and Street Name (include St., Ave., Rd., Ct., etc.).
   123 Main St.

Apt./Suite No. 6E or PO Box No. or ☐RR/ ☐HCR *(Check one)* RR/HCR Box No.

City Santa Maria State CA ZIP Code 94612 ZIP+4 8057

8a. For Puerto Rico Only: If NEW mailing address is in Puerto Rico, print urbanization name, if appropriate.

8b. Print NEW mailing address: House/Building Number and Street Name (include St., Ave., Rd., Ct., etc.).
   2914 Jerome Ave

Apt./Suite No. 1F or PO Box No. or ☐RR/ ☐HCR *(Check one)* RR/HCR Box No.

City Bronx State NY ZIP Code 10462 ZIP+4 6857

9. Sign and Print Name (see conditions on reverse)
   Sign: John T. Lee
   Print: John T. Lee

10. Date Signed: Month 01 Day 09 Year 00

OFFICIAL USE ONLY Verification Endorsement

PS FORM 3575

See http://www.usps.gov/moversnet for more information.

9096

Write with a Partner

Partner's Name _____

Answer these questions. • *Compare your answers with another pair of students.*

1. Whose application for a change of address is this? _____

2. What is his old mailing address? _____

   _____

3. What is his new mailing address? _____

   _____

4. When is the family moving? _____

CHANGE OF ADDRESS, p. 2

Class Brainstorm

Make a list on the board of people, institutions, and businesses you should notify if your address changes.

Write with a Partner

Partner's Name _____

Write your own list. Include real people, businesses, and institutions to notify if you move. • Read your list to a partner. • Compare your lists.

Print

Fill in the **Change of Address Order** for one of the people, businesses, or institutions on your list.

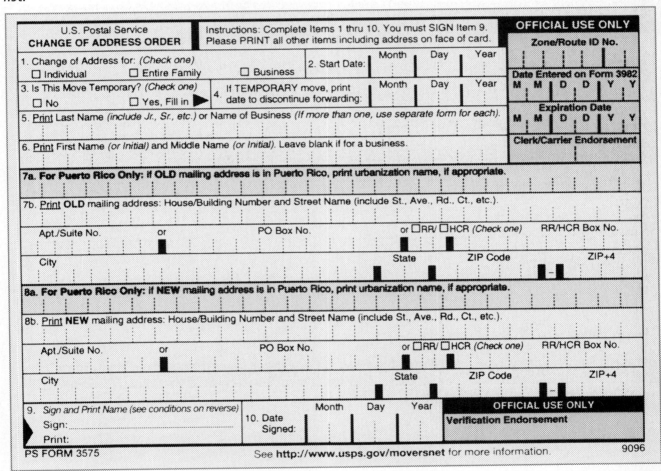

EXPRESS MAIL

Class Brainstorm

Did anyone in your class ever use an express mail service? • If so, tell what you sent and why you used the service. • List on the board situations that require an express mail service.

Write with the Class

Choose one situation. • Read this US Postal Service Express Mail label together, and fill it in for the situation.

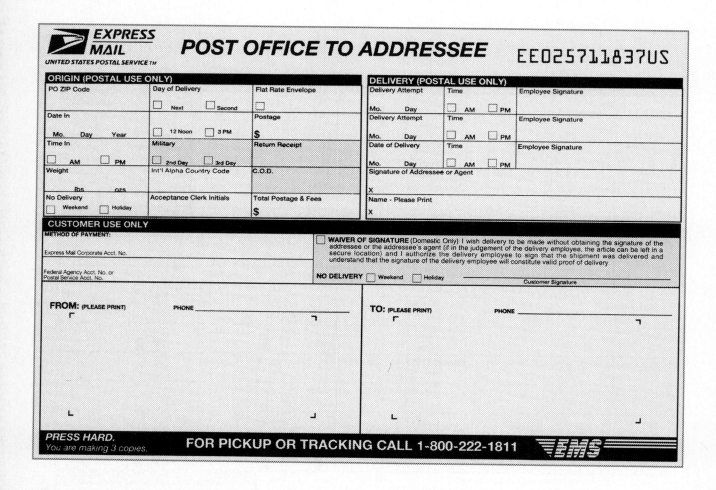

NOTES AND MESSAGES

SPELLING HINT

➤ When a word is only **1 syllable** long, has **1 vowel,** and **ends in 1 consonant,** double the consonant before adding **ing,** except after **w** or **x.**

run/running	stop/stopping	dig/digging
sit/sitting	rub/rubbing	sew/sewing
swim/swimming	cut/cutting	fix/fixing

DAILY PLANNER

Write

Fill in this schedule with your plans for tomorrow.

Daily Planner

Day: _____   Date: _____

6:00 AM _____	4:00 PM _____
7:00 AM _____	5:00 PM _____
8:00 AM _____	6:00 PM _____
9:00 AM _____	7:00 PM _____
10:00 AM _____	8:00 PM _____
11:00 AM _____	9:00 PM _____
12:00 PM _____	10:00 PM _____
1:00 PM _____	11:00 PM _____
2:00 PM _____	12:00 AM _____
3:00 PM _____	1:00 AM _____

Read With a Group

In groups of four, read your plans for tomorrow. • *Compare your schedules.*

Write

Write a schedule for your activities and appointments every day for a week.

NOTES TO YOURSELF

Group Survey

In groups of four, choose a recorder. • *Answer these questions.* • *Report your answers to the class.*

1. Do you write notes to yourself?
2. In what language do you write the notes?
3. In what situations do you write notes?
4. Are your notes short or long?
5. Do you write your notes on paper? in a book? another place?

Write with the Class

Write a list on the board of situations in which you write notes to yourselves.

Write

Write a "To Do" note to yourself about something you have to do.

Class Game: What Do You Remember?

Read your note to the class. • *Listen carefully to everyone's notes.* • *Remember as much as you can.* • *Make a list on the board of what everyone has to do.*

Write

Every day for a week, write notes to yourself in English.

TELEPHONE MESSAGES

Group Brainstorm
In groups of three or four, make a list of people who call you. • *Read your list to the class.*

Write with a Partner

Partner's Name _____

With your class, add more choices. • *Then complete these telephone messages with a partner.*

1. Your partner's name
2. Choose one:
   • *Your mother*
   • *Your teacher*
   • other:

   _____

3. Choose a time
4. Choose one:
   • *call back tonight*
   • *pick her up at 7:00*
   • *remember that class for tomorrow is cancelled*
   • other:

   _____

5. Your signature

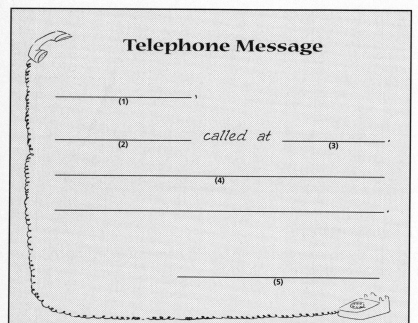

1. Your partner's name
2. Choose one:
   • *The doctor*
   • *The dentist*
   • *The babysitter*
   • other:

   _____

3. Choose a time
4. Choose one:
   • *Please call back*
   • *Your appointment is confirmed*
   • *She wants to talk to you*
   • other:

   _____

5. Your signature

TELEPHONE MESSAGES, p. 2

Write with a Partner

Partner's Name _____

With a partner, write a telephone conversation asking to speak to someone. • Take a message. • Read your conversation and your message to the class.

Telephone Message

Caller: _____ **Date:** _____ **Time:** _____

Please call back. Yes ☐ No ☐

Telephone Number: _____

Message: _____

_____

_____

_____

_____

Signed: _____

ABSENCE AND LATE NOTES

Class Brainstorm
List on the board acceptable reasons for a child to be absent from school or late to school.

Write
With your class, add more choices. • Then fill in this note to your child's teacher.

Dear _____ (1)

Dear _____ , (2)

_____ was (3)

_____ _____ (4)   (5)

because of _____ (6)

_____ .

Sincerely,

_____ (7)

1. Today's date
2. Your child's teacher's name
3. Your child's name
4. Choose one:
   • *absent*
   • *late*
5. Choose one:
   • *this morning*
   • *yesterday*
   • *last week*
   • *other:*

   _____

6. Choose one:
   • *a family obligation*
   • *a death in the family*
   • *a doctor's appointment*
   • *other:*

   _____

7. Your signature

Read with the Class
Read your notes to the class. • Which notes give good reasons for an excused absence?

Cross-Cultural Exchange
Are absence and late notes required in your country? • Tell the class about the customs.

EARLY DISMISSAL NOTES

Class Brainstorm

List on the board acceptable reasons for a child to leave school early. • List acceptable reasons for <u>you</u> to leave school early yourself. • Are there any differences between the two lists? • What are the differences?

Write

With your class, add more choices. • Then fill in this early dismissal note.

_____ (1)

Dear _____ (2) ,

Please dismiss _____ (3) at _____ (4) today because of _____ (5) .

Sincerely,

_____ (6)

1. Today's date
2. Your child's teacher's name
3. Your child's name
4. Choose one:
   • *10:00 AM*
   • *1:30 PM*
   • *noon*
   • other:

   _____

5. Choose one:
   • *a dentist's appointment*
   • *a doctor's appointment*
   • other:

   _____

6. Your signature

Write with a Group

Write a note to your child's teacher for early dismissal. • Read it to your group. • Edit the note. • Read your best note to the class.

PERMISSION SLIPS

Class Brainstorm

List on the board good field trip destinations. • Which field trips are especially good for children?

Write

With your class, add more choices. • Then fill in this permission slip.

To the Teacher,

_____ (1)

_____ (2) has my permission to accompany the class to the _____ (3) on _____ (4), _____ (5).

Sincerely,

_____ (6)

1. Today's date
2. Your child's name
3. Choose one:
   • *fire station*
   • *Science Museum*
   • *zoo*
   • other:

   _____

4. A day of the week
5. The date
6. Your signature

Write with a Partner   Partner's Name _____

Decide on a situation. • Write a permission note with your partner. • Read your note to another pair of students. • Edit the notes. • Read the notes to the class.

NOTES TO THE TEACHER

Write

With your class, add more choices. • Then complete these notes.

_____ (1)

Dear _____ (2) ,

I would like to meet with you to discuss

_____ (3)

_____ . I can come any

_____ (4) .

Sincerely,

_____ (5)

1. Date
2. Teacher's name
3. Choose one:
   • *a personal problem*
   • *my last test results*
   • *my future plans*
   • *my son's (daughter's) schoolwork*
   • other:

   _____

4. Choose one:
   • *Monday afternoon*
   • *Wednesday morning*
   • *Friday*
   • other:

   _____

5. Your signature

_____ (1)

Dear _____ (2) ,

I am leaving my _____ (3)

_____ . Please call me

at home if you have any questions. My

number is _____ (4) .

Sincerely,

_____ (5)

1. Date
2. Teacher's name
3. Choose one:
   • *homework*
   • *paper*
   • *test*
   • other:

   _____

4. Your telephone number
5. Your signature

Class Game: Guess Who

Write a note to your teacher. • Don't sign your name. • Fold the note. • Put each note on the teacher's desk. • Ask your teacher to read each note to the class. • Guess who wrote each one.

MAKING SIGNS

Print with a Partner

Partner's Name _____

With a partner, decide which sign is best for each situation. • Copy the words from the signs on the correct line below.

Situations

1. You need to sell your car: _____

2. The toilet is leaking and it floods the bathroom every time someone uses it:

   _____

3. The coffee machine in the lunch room is broken: _____

4. An apartment is vacant in the building where you are the superintendent:

   _____

5. A classmate is returning to class after being sick for a month: _____

   _____

MAKING SIGNS, p. 2

Print with a Partner

Partner's Name _____

Print signs for these situations. • *Show your signs to the class.*

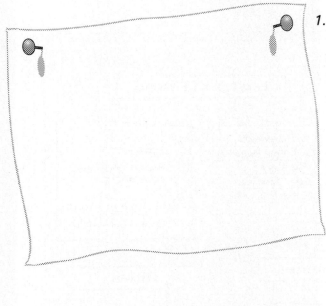

1. *Situation: Today is your teacher's birthday.*

2. *Situation: Smoking is not allowed in this area.*

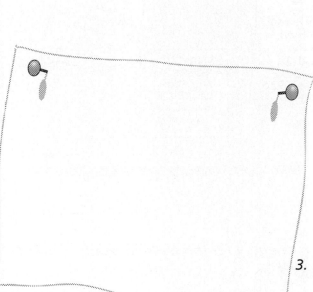

3. *Situation: Your baby is sleeping and will wake up if someone rings the doorbell.*

Class Project

With your class, decide on signs to make for your classroom. • *Design them together.* • *Make the signs.* • *Hang them up.*

Community Activity

What signs do you see in your community? • *Copy one.* • *Bring it to class.* • *Explain it to the class.* • *Make a collage of all the community signs.*

NOTES FOR A BULLETIN BOARD

Read with the Class

Read the notes and notices on this bulletin board. • What different kinds of notices are there?

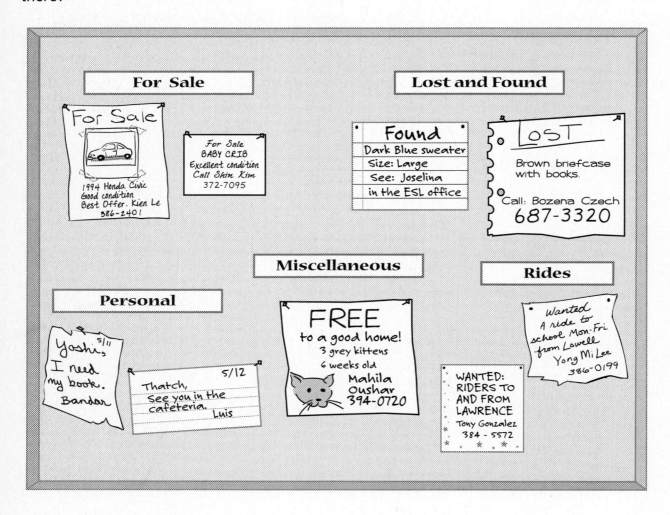

Group Brainstorm

In groups of three, list other possible items in each category for this bulletin board. • Read your list to the class. • Write the class list on the board.

Read with a Partner   Partner's Name _____

With a partner, find a bulletin board in your school. • Read the notices on the board. • What kinds of notes and notices are there? • Make a list. • Report to your class.

NOTES FOR A BULLETIN BOARD, p. 2

Write with a Partner

Partner's Name _____

With a partner, write notes for these bulletin boards. • *Read your notes to another pair of students.*

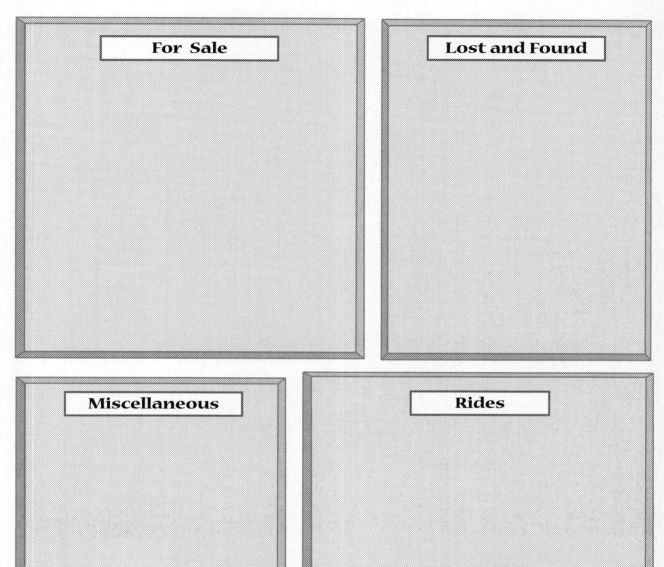

For Sale

Lost and Found

Miscellaneous

Rides

Write with the Class

Make a bulletin board for your class. • *Include at least three categories.* • *Write notes or notices and post them on the board.* • *Check the board every time you go to class.*

Community Activity

Find bulletin boards in the supermarket, community center, and post office. • *List categories, and then list the kinds of notices you find.* • *Compare your lists in class.*

CANCELLATION AND POSTPONEMENT NOTICES

Class Brainstorm

List on the board events that are sometimes cancelled. • *List reasons to **cancel** (no new date)
or **postpone** (reschedule for a later date) an event.*

Write

With your class, add more choices. • *Then complete these notes.*

The _____ (1)

The _____ (2) that
was scheduled for today at
_____ (3) is cancelled due
to _____ (4) .

1. Today's date
2. Choose one:
   • *class*
   • *club meeting*
   • *tenants' meeting*
   • *other:* _____
3. Choose a time
4. Choose one:
   • *snow*
   • *illness*
   • *a leaky pipe*
   • *other:* _____

_____ (1)

The _____ (2)
that was scheduled for today at
_____ (3) is postponed due to
_____ (4) . It will be
rescheduled for _____ (5)
_____ .

1. Today's date
2. Choose one:
   • *class*
   • *club meeting*
   • *tenants' meeting*
   • *other:* _____
3. Choose a time
4. Choose one:
   • *snow*
   • *illness*
   • *a leaky pipe*
   • *other:* _____
5. Choose one:
   • *next week at the same time*
   • *Monday at 4:00 p.m.*
   • *next month at the same time*
   • *other:*

_____

Print with the Class

Decide on a reason to cancel your class. • *Print a class cancellation note on the board.*

Print with a Partner   Partner's Name _____

A film for your class is postponed from tomorrow at 1:00 p.m. to next Monday at 2:00. • *Print
the postponement notice with a partner.*

UNIT 6

INVITATIONS AND THANK-YOU NOTES

SPELLING HINT

➤ When a word ends in a **consonant + y,** change **y** to **i** before adding **ed** or **es,** but keep the **y** before adding the ending **ing.**

c**ry**/c**ried**/c**ries**/cr**ying**   play/play**ed**/play**s**/play**ing**

f**ry**/f**ried**/f**ries**/fr**ying**   stay/stay**ed**/stay**s**/stay**ing**

sp**y**/sp**ied**/sp**ies**/sp**ying**   enjoy/enjoy**ed**/enjoy**s**/enjoy**ing**

BIRTHDAY PARTY INVITATIONS

Write with a Partner

Partner's Name _____

With a partner, decide on answers to each question. • *Then write your answers.* • *Compare your answers with the class.*

1. Whose birthday is it? _____

2. What is the date for the party? _____

3. What time will the party begin? _____

4. Where will the party be? _____

5. What telephone number will guests call in order to respond? _____

Write with a Partner

With the same partner, fill in the birthday party invitation.

A Birthday Party for

_____
(1)

Date: _____
(2)

Time: _____
(3)

Where: _____
(4)

_____

Call: _____
(5)

Class Game: Respond!

Put all the invitations in a pile. • *Choose one with your partner.* • *Role play your decision to go to the party or not.* • *Call the telephone number to accept or refuse the invitation.* • *Talk with the pair who wrote the invitation.*

Write with the Class

With your class, draw an invitation form on the board. • *Write an invitation for your families and friends to come to an open house in your classroom.* • *Copy the invitation.* • *Give invitations to your families and friends.*

INVITE A FRIEND

Class Brainstorm

List on the board special occasions when you would invite a friend.

Write with a Partner

Partner's Name _____

Add more choices. • *Then fill in this invitation to your partner.* • *Read your invitation to your partner.*

_____ (1)

Dear _____ , (2)

_____ to (3)

_____ (4)

_____ (5)

on _____ . Please _____ . (6) (7)

_____ .

My telephone number is _____ . (8)

Sincerely,

_____ (9)

1. Date
2. Your partner's name
3. Choose one:
   - *You're invited*
   - *Please come*
   - *I'd like to invite you*
   - other:

   _____

4. Choose one:
   - *a New Year's party*
   - *visit me*
   - *a class get-together*
   - other:

   _____

5. Choose one:
   - *on your vacation*
   - *the last day of class*
   - *for the weekend*
   - other:

   _____

6. Choose a date.
7. Choose one:
   - *call me*
   - *let me know if you can come*
   - *say Yes!*
   - other:

   _____

8. Your telephone number
9. Your signature

LETTER OF ACCEPTANCE

Write with a Partner

Partner's Name _____

With your class, add more choices. • *Write a letter of acceptance to your partner.*

_____ (1)

Dear _____ (2) ,

Thank you for inviting me to

_____ (3)

_____ .

I _____ (4)

_____ .

I'm looking forward to seeing you then!

_____ (5) ,

_____ (6)

1. Date
2. Name of person who invited you
3. Choose one:
   • *your home*
   • *your surprise party*
   • *the class get-together*
   • *other:*

   _____

4. Choose one:
   • *will be happy to come*
   • *am delighted to accept*
   • *will be glad to be there*
   • *will certainly be there*
   • *other:*

   _____

5. Choose one:
   • *Your friend*
   • *Sincerely*
   • *Best regards*
   • *other:*

   _____

6. Your signature

Write with the Class

Put all the letters of acceptance in a pile. • *Choose one.* • *Write an invitation for your letter of acceptance.* • *Read it to the class.*

LETTER OF REGRET

Class Brainstorm

List on the board good reasons to decline an invitation. • *How can you decline politely if you don't want to or can't accept?*

Write with a Partner

Partner's Name _____

With your class, add more choices. • *Write a letter of regret to your partner.*

_____ (1)

Dear _____ (2) *,*

Thank you for inviting me to

_____ (3) *.*

_____ (4)

I won't be able to _____ (5)

_____ *because* (6)

_____ (6)

_____ (7) *,*

_____ (8)

1. Date
2. Your partner's name
3. Choose one:
   • *your New Year's party*
   • *visit you*
   • *the class get-together*
   • other:

   _____

4. Choose one:
   • *Unfortunately,*
   • *I'm sorry that*
   • *I'm disappointed that*
   • other:

   _____

5. Choose one:
   • *accept*
   • *attend*
   • *be with you*
   • other:

   _____

6. Choose one:
   • *I'm going to be away*
   • *I have a previous commitment*
   • *I have to work on that day*
   • other:

   _____

7. Choose one:
   • *Your friend*
   • *Sincerely*
   • *Best regards*
   • other:

   _____

8. Your signature

WEDDING INVITATION

Read with the Class

Read this formal wedding invitation. • *Who is sending the invitation?* • *Who is the bride? the groom?* • *When and where is the ceremony?*

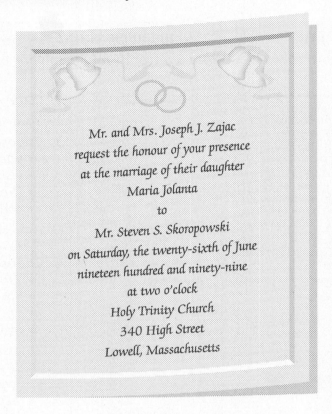

Mr. and Mrs. Joseph J. Zajac
request the honour of your presence
at the marriage of their daughter
Maria Jolanta
to
Mr. Steven S. Skoropowski
on Saturday, the twenty-sixth of June
nineteen hundred and ninety-nine
at two o'clock
Holy Trinity Church
340 High Street
Lowell, Massachusetts

Write

Fill in the response card for this wedding.

Reception
at three o'clock
Nat Sergi's Joseph's Lounge
Lowell, Massachusetts

Please respond on or before
June 12, 1999.

M _____

will _____ attend.

will not _____ attend.

Cross-Cultural Exchange

For what events do people send formal invitations in your country? • *What do people wear to weddings in your country?* • *Do you have any wedding pictures from your country?* • *Show them to the class and describe the wedding.*

RESPONSE TO FORMAL INVITATIONS

Read with the Class

Read this formal invitation. • *What is this invitation for?* • *What will the celebration include?*

You are cordially invited to attend
the 25th Wedding Anniversary celebration of
Tony and Rowena Moreno,
Friday, January 8th, 1999,
at 3:00p.m.
St. Bernard's Church, Pirtleville, AZ.
Reception Douglas Golf Club, Douglas, AZ at 4:30

Write

With your class, add more choices. • *Then complete this letter of acceptance to the formal invitation.*

_____
(1)

Dear _____,
(2)
Thank you for the invitation to your

_____.
(3)

I _____.
(4)

I'm looking forward to spending the day

with you.

_____,
(5)

_____
(6)

1. Date
2. Name of the person who sent the invitation
3. Name of the occasion
4. Choose one:
   • *am happy to accept*
   • *accept your invitation*
   • *gladly accept*
   • other:

   _____

5. Choose one:
   • *Sincerely*
   • *Yours truly*
   • *Warm regards*
   • other:

   _____

6. Your signature

RESPONSE TO FORMAL INVITATIONS, p. 2

Write

Now decline the invitation with a letter of regret. • *First add more choices.* • *Then fill in the letter.*

_____ (1)

Dear _____ (2) ,

_____ (3) I will not be

able to attend your _____ (4)

_____

I _____ (5)

_____ .

_____ (6)

_____

_____ (7) ,

_____ (8)

1. Date
2. Name of the person who sent you the invitation
3. Choose one:
   - *I'm sorry*
   - *I regret*
   - *Unfortunately,*
   - other:

   _____

4. Name of the occasion
5. Choose one:
   - *have to work that day*
   - *made previous plans*
   - *have friends coming to visit me that day*
   - other:

   _____

6. Choose one:
   - *I'll be thinking of you on that day.*
   - *I'll be in touch soon.*
   - *Best wishes!*
   - other:

   _____

7. Choose one:
   - *Sincerely*
   - *Love*
   - *Best regards*
   - other:

   _____

8. Your signature

INVITATION TO AN HONORED GUEST

Class Brainstorm
List on the board special events at school and special guests to invite.

Write with a Group
In groups of three, add more choices. • *Then fill in this invitation.*

_____ (1)

_____

_____ (2)

_____ (3)

_____ (4)

_____

Dear _____ (5) ,

_____ (6)

would like to invite you to its _____ (7)

_____,

on _____ (8) .

We would be honored to have you _____ (9)

_____.

Sincerely,

_____ (10) ,

_____ (11)

_____

1. Address of your school
2. Today's date
3. Choose one:
   • Name of a city or town official
   • Name of a school administrator
   • Name of a famous person
   • other:

   _____

4. Address of the guest
5. Title and last name of guest
6. Choose one:
   • *Our ESL class*
   • *The International Club*
   • *The Foreign Students' Club*
   • other:

   _____

7. Choose one:
   • *International dinner*
   • *Graduation ceremony*
   • *Open house*
   • other:

   _____

8. Choose a date.
9. Choose one:
   • *come as our guest*
   • *address our group*
   • *distribute the awards*
   • *award the diplomas*
   • other:

   _____

10. Your signature
11. Choose one:
    • *Secretary, ESL Class*
    • *Representative, International Club*
    • *Representative, Foreign Students' Club*
    • other:

    _____

THANK-YOU NOTE FOR A GIFT

Class Brainstorm

List occasions on the board when you would write a thank-you note.

Write

With your class, add more choices. • *Then complete this thank-you note.*

```
_____
                        (1)


Dear _____,
            (2)

_____ for the gift
            (3)

you sent me _____
                      (4)

_____. It's

_____
            (5)

_____.

I really _____ the
              (6)

_____.
            (7)

_____,
            (8)

_____
            (9)
```

1. Date
2. Name of a friend or relative
3. Choose one:
   • *Thanks*
   • *Thank you*
   • *Many thanks*
4. Choose one:
   • *on my graduation*
   • *on my birthday*
   • *when I was sick*
   • *other:* _____
5. Choose one:
   • *beautiful*
   • *perfect*
   • *just what I wanted*
   • *other:* _____
6. Choose one:
   • *appreciate*
   • *like*
   • *love*
7. Choose one:
   • *CD*
   • *book*
   • *flowers*
   • *other:* _____
8. Choose one:
   • *Love*
   • *Fondly*
   • *Sincerely*
   • *other:* _____
9. Your signature

Class Game: Thank you!

Write the name of a gift on a slip of paper. • *Include your name.* • *Fold the paper.* • *Put all the slips in a pile.* • *Pick a paper.* • *Imagine that you received the gift.* • *Write a thank-you note for the gift.* • *Read your note to the student whose slip of paper you chose.*

Cross-Cultural Exchange

How do you write "thank you" in your language? • *Do you know how to say "thank you" in another language?* • *Write all the ways on the board.* • *Teach the class the pronunciation.* • *What are the customs in your country about written thank-you notes?* • *When is it appropriate to send written thank-you notes?*

THANK-YOU NOTE FOR A VISIT

Write

With your class, add more choices. • *Then complete this thank-you note.*

_____ (1)

Dear _____ (2) ,

_____ (3) with you

_____ (4) was

_____ (5) !

I especially enjoyed _____ (6)

_____ .

Thank you for inviting me and for your hospitality.

_____ (7) ,

_____ (8)

1. Date
2. Name of a friend or relative
3. Choose one:
   • *My visit*
   • *Visiting*
   • *Staying*
   • other:

   _____

4. Choose one:
   • *last week*
   • *last weekend*
   • *last month*
   • other:

   _____

5. Choose one:
   • *wonderful*
   • *a lot of fun*
   • *great*
   • other:

   _____

6. Choose one:
   • *your mother's cooking*
   • *the walks we took*
   • *just being with you and your family*
   • other:

   _____

7. Choose one:
   • *Love*
   • *Fondly*
   • *With best regards*
   • other:

   _____

8. Your signature

Write with a Partner   Partner's Name _____

Discuss this situation with a partner: You moved to a new town. Friends let you stay with them until you found an apartment. You stayed with them for a week. • *Write a telephone conversation and thank your friends.* • *Read your conversation to the class.*

THANK-YOU NOTE FOR HELP

Class Brainstorm

List on the board kinds of help people give to each other. • In which situations would you write a thank-you note?

Write

With your class, add more choices. Then complete this note.

_____ (1)

Dear _____ (2) ,

Thank you for _____ (3)
_____ .

I really appreciate your taking the
time to _____ (4) .

_____ (5) ,

_____ (6)

1. Date
2. Name of the person who helped you
3. Choose one:
   - *helping me*
   - *the help you have given me*
   - *working with me*
   - *other:*

   _____

4. Choose one:
   - *study with me*
   - *talk with me*
   - *advise me*
   - *do so much for me*
   - *other:*

   _____

5. Choose one:
   - *Sincerely*
   - *Your friend*
   - *Your student*
   - *other:*

   _____

6. Your signature

Write

Write a thank-you note to someone who has helped you. • Send the note. • If you get a response, share it with the class.

HOME AND HEALTH

SPELLING HINT

➤ The **long a sound** is usually spelled **a (consonant) e**, or **ai**, or **ay**.

s**a**v**e**	w**ai**t	m**ay**
sk**a**t**e**	r**ai**n	st**ay**
pl**a**t**e**	br**ai**n	aw**ay**

SALAD RECIPES

Group Brainstorm

In groups of four, list salad ingredients. • *Read your list to the class.* • *Make a class list on the board.*

Write with a Partner

Partner's Name _____

With the class, add more choices. • *Work with a partner to complete this recipe for a salad.*

Recipe for Garden Salad

_____ (1)   _____ (2)

_____ .

into small pieces and put in bowl. Add _____ (3)

_____

_____ .

Top with _____ (4)

_____ .

Serve with _____ (5) dressing.

1. Choose one:
   • *Tear*
   • *Slice*
   • *Shred*

2. Choose one or more:
   • *romaine lettuce*
   • *iceberg lettuce*
   • *cabbage*
   • other:

   _____

3. Choose as many as you like:
   • *cucumber slices*
   • *chopped green pepper*
   • *chopped scallions*
   • other:

   _____

4. Choose as many as you like:
   • *croutons*
   • *cheese*
   • *alfalfa sprouts*
   • other:

   _____

5. Choose one:
   • *Thousand Island*
   • *Italian*
   • *oil and vinegar*
   • other:

   _____

Community Activity

Write a shopping list of all the ingredients in this salad recipe. • *Take your list to a market and look for all the ingredients.* • *Check off the ingredients you find.* • *Note prices.* • *How much will it cost to prepare your salad?* • *Report to the class.*

Cross-Cultural Exchange

What kinds of salads do people eat in your country? • *Write other recipes and make an international salad book with your class.*

SOUP RECIPES

Write with the Class

List on the board the kinds of soup that you like. • Copy the list in your notebook.

Write

Decide what kind of soup you will make. • Add more choices. • Complete this recipe for soup.

RECIPE FOR: _____

Ingredients:

_____ (1)   _____ (1)

_____   _____

Instructions:

(2)

the ingredients and place them in a pot with
.

(3)

Bring to a boil. Reduce the heat. Simmer for
.

(4)

1. Choose four or more:
   - *rice*
   - *noodles*
   - *potatoes*
   - *carrots*
   - *onions*
   - *beans*
   - *lentils*
   - *chicken*
   - *tomatoes*
   - *celery*
   - *corn*
   - other:

   _____

2. Choose as many as you want:
   - *Wash*
   - *Cut*
   - *Peel*
   - *Soak*
   - other:

   _____

3. Choose as many as you want:
   - *water*
   - *chicken broth*
   - *bouillon*
   - *pepper*
   - *parsley*
   - other:

   _____

4. Choose one:
   - *one hour*
   - *two hours*
   - other:

   _____

Cross-Cultural Exchange

Do people make soup for special occasions in your country? • Do people make special soup for someone who is sick? • Do you ever have soup when you are sick? • What kinds?

DESSERT RECIPES

Read with the Class

Read this recipe for Apple Crisp. • What are the ingredients? • What are the instructions?

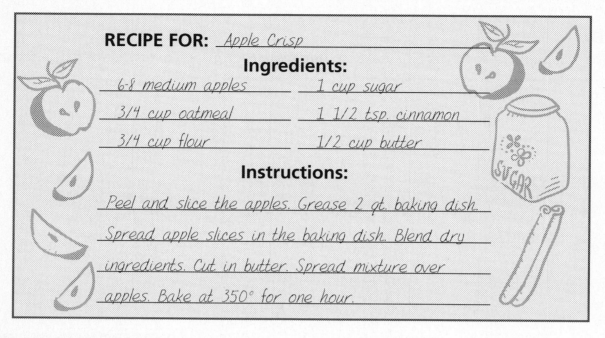

RECIPE FOR: _Apple Crisp_

Ingredients:

6-8 medium apples	1 cup sugar
3/4 cup oatmeal	1 1/2 tsp. cinnamon
3/4 cup flour	1/2 cup butter

Instructions:

Peel and slice the apples. Grease 2 qt. baking dish. Spread apple slices in the baking dish. Blend dry ingredients. Cut in butter. Spread mixture over apples. Bake at 350° for one hour.

Write with a Group

In groups of three, describe your favorite dessert recipe. • Explain the ingredients and the instructions. • Choose one recipe to write together. • Copy your recipe on the board. • Copy all the groups' recipes from the board into the Activities section of your notebook.

RECIPE FOR: _____

Ingredients:

_____   _____

_____   _____

_____

Instructions:

_____

_____

_____

_____

_____

MENU PLANNING

Write with the Class

List on the board foods you eat everyday.   •   Then look at the food pyramid shown below.   •
Where does each of the foods you eat belong in the pyramid?

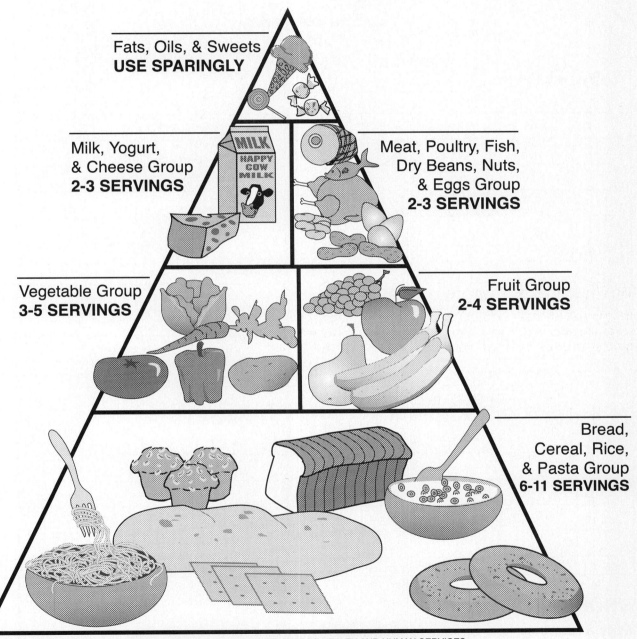

Fats, Oils, & Sweets
USE SPARINGLY

Milk, Yogurt,
& Cheese Group
2-3 SERVINGS

Meat, Poultry, Fish,
Dry Beans, Nuts,
& Eggs Group
2-3 SERVINGS

Vegetable Group
3-5 SERVINGS

Fruit Group
2-4 SERVINGS

Bread,
Cereal, Rice,
& Pasta Group
6-11 SERVINGS

Source: U.S. DEPARTMENT OF AGRICULTURE and the U.S. DEPARTMENT OF HEALTH AND HUMAN SERVICES.

MENU PLANNING, p. 2

Write with a Group

In groups of four, prepare a one-day menu for your group. • Include food from all food groups in the pyramid. • Compare your menu with another group's menu. • Which group had the most balanced diet?

Menu for Today

Breakfast

_____   _____
_____   _____
_____   _____
_____   _____

Lunch

_____   _____
_____   _____
_____   _____
_____   _____

Dinner

_____   _____
_____   _____
_____   _____
_____   _____

Write

Write a recipe for one of your favorite foods. • Bring your recipe to class.

Class Project

Make a class book of all the recipes. • Make copies of the book for everyone in the class. • Have a class party. • Use some of the recipes to prepare food at home and bring it to class. • Sample all the different foods. • Enjoy!

SUPERMARKET SHOPPING LIST

Class Brainstorm

List on the board things you buy.

1. in boxes
2. in cans
3. in bottles
4. in bunches
5. in plastic containers
6. in jars
7. in pounds
8. other: _____

_____

Copy the lists in the Vocabulary section of your notebook.

Write with a Partner

Finish this shopping list with your partner.

1 bunch of
1 package of
1 loaf of
3 jars of
1 box of
2 bottles of
1 container of
1 pound of
2 cans of
1 dozen

Write

Write a shopping list of the things you and your family buy at the supermarket. • *If you do not know the English words for some foods, write them in your language.*

Cross-Cultural Exchange

Do you have any of the same things on your list? • *What are they?* • *What is on your list?* • *Did anyone write a bilingual shopping list?* • *If so, which food items did you list in each language?* • *Can you buy ethnic food in your neighborhood?* • *Where?* • *Which food?*

SAVING MONEY WITH COUPONS

Read with the Class

Answer these questions about coupons.

1. Where are these coupons from? What are they for?
2. What is the difference between a store coupon and a manufacturer's coupon?
3. What are the expiration dates on these coupons?
4. What are the limits?
5. How much money can you save on the canned chicken?
6. How much does each bottle of DP Cola cost with the coupon?

Community Activity

Bring to class coupons from supermarket ads, newspaper supplements, and supermarket coupon books. • Read the coupons together. • Plan a party for your class. • Which coupons can you use?

Write with a Partner   Partner's Name _____

With a partner, write a shopping list for the class party. • Include everything you will need to buy. • Read your list to the class. • Make a class list.

Class Project

Have a party. • Collect money. • Buy the party food and supplies. • Have fun!

COMPARISON SHOPPING

Read with a Group

In groups of four, compare these ads. • Answer the questions. • Then report your answers to the class.

1. What fruits are the best buy this week?
2. What is an inexpensive way to buy chicken? Why?
3. Is the store brand or the national brand cheaper for ice cream?
4. Which items are better buys at Supermart? At Savemore?
5. Which supermarket has the better prices in general?

Write with a Partner   Partner's Name _____

With a partner, choose one of the two supermarkets. • Write a shopping list with four items from the ad. • Include quantities and total cost. • Read your list to another pair of students.

Shopping List					
Quantity	Item	Cost	Quantity	Item	Cost
_____	_____	_____	_____	_____	_____
_____	_____	_____	_____	_____	_____

RENTAL AGREEMENT

Read with the Class

Read this rental agreement. • What does each section mean?

RESIDENTIAL LEASE

LEASE AGREEMENT, entered into between _____ (Landlord) and
_____ (Tenant).

For good consideration it is agreed between the parties as follows:

1. Landlord hereby leases and lets to Tenant the premises described as follows:

2. This lease shall be for a term of _____ year(s), commencing on _____,
    _____.
    [Year]   [Date]

3. Tenant shall pay Landlord the annual rent of $_____ during said term, in
    monthly payments of $_____, each payable monthly on the first day of each
    month in advance. Tenant shall pay a security deposit of $_____, to be returned
    upon termination of this Lease and the payment of all rents due and performance of
    all other obligations.

4. Tenant shall at its own expense provide the following utilities or services:
    _____ _____. Landlord shall at its expense

    provide the following utilities or services: _____.

5. Tenant further agrees that:

    a) Upon the expiration of the Lease it shall return possession of the leased premises
    in its present condition, reasonable wear and tear, fire casualty excepted.

    b) Tenant shall not assign or sublet said premises or allow any other person to occupy
    the leased premises without Landlord's prior written consent.

    c) Tenant shall not make any material or structural alterations to the leased premises
    without Landlord's prior written consent.

    d) Tenant shall comply with all building, zoning and health codes and other
    applicable laws for the use of said premises.

    e) Tenant shall not conduct on premises any activity deemed extra hazardous, or a
    nuisance, or requiring an increase in fire insurance premiums.

    f) Tenant shall not allow pets on the premises.

    g) In the event of any breach of the payment of rent or any other allowed charge, or
    other breach of this Lease, Landlord shall have full rights to terminate this Lease in
    accordance with state law and re-enter and re-claim possession of the leased premises,
    in addition to such other remedies available to Landlord arising from said breach.

Signed this _____ day of _____ _____.
In the presence of: [Year]

_____ _____ Witness Landlord

_____ _____ Witness Tenant

RENTAL AGREEMENT, p. 2

Write with a Group

In groups of three, fill out the rental agreement.

Write with a Group

In the same groups, write a conversation between a realtor and two prospective tenants. •
Ask and answer questions about a rental agreement. • Read your conversation to the class.

Partner Interview   Partner's Name _____

Ask a partner these questions. • Write your partner's answers.

1. Do you rent your home? If so, what utilities are included in your rent?
2. When is your rent due? What happens if your rent is late?
3. Do you have a lease or other written rental agreement? What is the term of your agreement?
4. Did you have to pay a security deposit when you moved in?
5. Who manages your rental? A landlord? A realty company?
6. Did you ever have a problem with a rental agreement? What happened?

Write with a Group

In groups of four, write as many questions about a rental agreement as you can. • Exchange
questions with another group. • Write answers to the other group's questions.

Cross-Cultural Exchange

In the same groups, discuss these questions.

1. In your country, do renters sign leases?
2. What is the usual length of the lease?
3. Do rental agreements require a security deposit? an advanced payment?
4. Do rental agreements ever include utilities? Which ones?
5. Who signs the agreement?
6. What happens if the tenant is in breach of the agreement? if the landlord is in breach?

HOUSING COMPLAINT

Class Brainstorm

Make a list on the board of housing problems. • *Which complaint is the most common?*

Write

With your class, add more choices. • *Then complete this housing complaint.* • *Remember to keep copies of the business letters you write!*

_____ (1)

Dear _____ (2) ,

I live at _____ (3) . I am

having a problem with _____ (4) .

Please contact me. My telephone number is

_____ (5) .

Thank you.

_____ (6)

1. Today's date
2. Name of your superintendent, agent, or landlord
3. Your address
4. Choose one:
   • *the sink*
   • *the heat*
   • *cockroaches*
   • *other:*

   _____

5. Your telephone number
6. Your signature

Write

If you don't get an answer, write another note. • *Add more choices.* • *Then fill in this follow-up complaint.*

_____ (1)

Dear _____ (2) ,

I contacted you last week about a problem with

_____ (3) . I have not yet

heard from you. Please get in touch with me

_____ (4) . The problem is

getting worse. If I do not hear from you soon, I will

have to take further action to solve my problem.

Sincerely,

_____ (5)

1. Today's date
2. Name of your superintendent, agent, or landlord
3. Kind of problem
4. Choose one:
   • *immediately*
   • *today*
   • *by Friday*
   • *other:*

   _____

5. Your signature

HOUSING COMPLAINT, p. 2

Community Activity

Find the title and address of the housing authority in your community. • *Copy it below.*

Write with a Partner   Partner's Name _____

If your landlord does not respond to your notes, write a letter to the housing authority to complain about your landlord.

_____ (1)

_____ (2)

_____ (3)

_____ (4)

_____ (5)

Dear Sir or Madam,

I contacted my _____ (6)

on _____ (7) about a problem

with _____ (8) .

My _____ (6) has not

responded and the problem is getting worse.

I would appreciate your help in this matter.

Sincerely,

_____ (9)

1. Your address
2. Your city, state, and zip code
3. Date
4. Exact name of local Housing Authority
5. Address of Housing Authority
6. Choose one:
   • *landlord*
   • *superintendent*
   • *agent*
   • other:

   _____

7. Date of first note
8. Name your problem
9. Your signature

Write with a Partner

With the same partner, write a telephone conversation between a landlord and a tenant about a housing complaint. • *Read your conversation to the class.*

SHOPPING FOR HOME REPAIR SUPPLIES

Group Brainstorm

In groups of three, list tools and supplies you would need for a tool kit to make home repairs. • Read your list to the class. • Then make a class list on the board.

Community Activity

Visit a local hardware store with your group. • Find the items on your home repair list and fill in the chart below. • Report your findings to the class.

Name of hardware store: _____

Item	Brand	Quantity	Cost
			$.
			$.
			$.
			$.
			$.
			$.
			$.
			$.
			$.
			$.
			$.
			$.
			$.
			$.
			$.
			$.
			$.

PHARMACY SHOPPING

Group Brainstorm

In groups of three, list items you would need for a first-aid kit. • *Read your list to the class.* • *Then make a class list on the board.*

Community Activity

Visit a local pharmacy with your group. • *Find the items on your first-aid kit list and fill in the chart below.* • *Report your findings to the class.*

Name of pharmacy: _____

Item	Brand	Size	Cost
			$.
			$.
			$.
			$.
			$.
			$.
			$.
			$.
			$.
			$.
			$.
			$.
			$.
			$.
			$.
			$.
			$.

HEALTH INSURANCE FORM

Read with the Class

Read this form. • *Discuss any new vocabulary.*

INSURANCE REGISTRATION FORM					
History #	NY Dr. Code	M.D. Name		Date	Registrar

PATIENT INFORMATION					
Patient Name		Social Security #		Sex M F	Account #
Address	Apt.	City		State	Zip Code
DOB / /	Place of Birth	Marital Status S M W D Sep	Race	Mother	Father	Home Phone ( )

EMPLOYER INFORMATION				
Employer				
Address	City		State	Zip Code
Occupation				Work Phone ( )

EMERGENCY CONTACT				
Name		Relationship		
Address	City		State	Zip Code
	Home Phone ( )		Work Phone ( )	

INSURANCE INFORMATION					
Insurance # 1	Code	Insured	Insured's Phone Number ( )		
		Policy #			
		Group #			Other #
Insurance # 2	Code	Insured	Insured's Phone Number ( )		
		Policy #			
		Group #			Other #

OTHER INFORMATION			
Referred by			
Address	City	State	Zip Code
Family Physician			
Address	City	State	Zip Code

I authorize any holder of medical or other information about me to release to the Social Security Administration and Health Care Financing Administration or its intermediaries or carriers; or to the billing agent of this physician or supplier which is Medical Services Division, any information needed for this or a related Medicare claim. I permit a copy of this authorization to be used in place of the original, and request payment of medical insurance benefits either to myself or to the party who accepts assignment. I certify that all information above is true and correct. I understand that I am responsible for any bills generated from services rendered.

Signature of Patient	Date / /	Signature of Responsible Person	Date / /

Print

Fill in this form with your own information.

Write with a Partner   Partner's Name _____

With a partner, write a conversation between a medical receptionist and a patient about health insurance. • *Read your conversation to another pair of students.*

TRAVEL

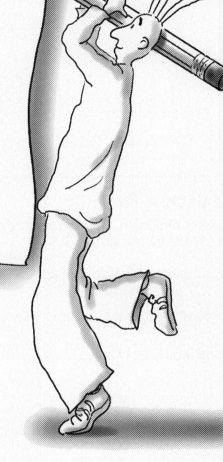

SPELLING HINT

➤ The **long e sound** is usually spelled **ee,** or **ea,** or **ie.**

d**ee**p	dr**ea**m	f**ie**ld
sl**ee**p	sp**ea**k	ch**ie**f
k**ee**p	l**ea**se	br**ie**f

GIVING DIRECTIONS

Read with the Class

Read this map with your class. • Then make up questions about the map.

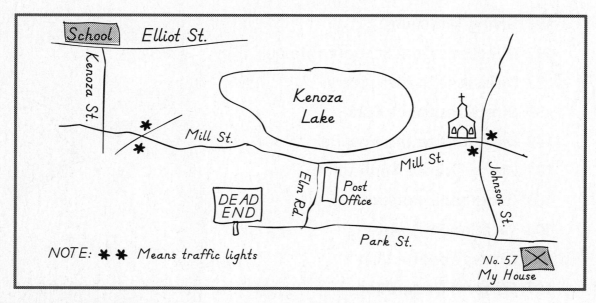

NOTE: ✱ ✱ Means traffic lights

Write with a Partner

Partner's Name _____

Write directions from the school to My House with a partner. • Check your directions with the class. • Are they the same?

Go down Kenoza Street. Turn _____ (1)
at the end onto _____ (2). Go through
_____ (3). At the lake turn
_____ (4) onto _____ (5)
_____. Go past the post office on the
_____ (6) and turn _____ (7)
onto Park Street. My house is number 57 on the
_____ (8) side of the street.

1. Choose one:
   • *left*   • *right*
2. Choose one:
   • *Elliot Street*
   • *Mill Street*
3. Choose one:
   • *Kenoza Lake*
   • *the traffic lights*
4. Choose one:
   • *left*   • *right*
5. Choose one:
   • *Johnson Street*
   • *Elm Road*
6. Choose one:
   • *left*   • *right*
7. Choose one:
   • *left*   • *right*
8. Choose one:
   • *left*   • *right*

DIRECTIONS FROM SCHOOL TO HOME

Print with a Partner   Partner's Name _____

Draw a map from your school to your home. • *Include traffic lights, important streets, and other landmarks.* • *Explain your map to a partner.*

From School to My Home

Write with a Partner   Partner's Name _____

Now write the directions to your home for the same partner. • *Include all the turns, all the traffic lights, important street names, and landmarks.* • *Have your partner read the directions.* • *Are they clear?* • *If not, improve them.*

Partner Interview

Ask the same partner these questions. • *Write your partner's answers in your notebook.*

1. How far from school do you live?
2. How long does it take you to get to school?
3. Do you make the trip to school by car, by bus, or on foot?
4. What street (road, avenue, etc.) do you live on?
5. What other buildings are on your street?
6. What landmarks are on your map?
7. What streets are on your map?
8. Please tell me how to get to your house from our school.

DIRECTIONS TO THE LIBRARY

Group Survey

In groups of five, choose a recorder. • *Ask everyone these questions.* • *Record the answers.* • *Report your group's answers to the class.*

	Yes	No
1. Do you ever go to a library?	_____	_____
2. Do you have a library card?	_____	_____
3. Do you know where the public library is in your community?	_____	_____
4. Do you like to read in the library?	_____	_____
5. Do you like to study in the library?	_____	_____
6. Do you take books out of the library?	_____	_____
7. Do you borrow language tapes from the library?	_____	_____
8. Do you borrow videotapes from the library?	_____	_____

Print with the Class

Make a map on the board to show how to go from school to the public library. • *Copy the map onto this page.*

From School to the Library

Community Activity

Go to the public library. • *Apply for a library card.* • *Bring along proof of residency in your community.* • *Borrow a book, audiotape, or videotape from the library.* • *Bring it to school and show it to your classmates.*

DIRECTIONS TO THE PARK

Partner Interview

Partner's Name _____

Ask your partner these questions. • *Write your partner's answers in your notebook.*

1. Is there a public park in your community?
2. What do people do at the park?
3. Is the park safe at night?
4. Is it near your home?
5. How often do you go to other parks?
6. Tell me about your favorite park.

Print with a Partner

Draw a map from your home to the park. • *Include important streets, traffic lights, and landmarks.* • *Explain your map to your partner.*

From My Home to the Park

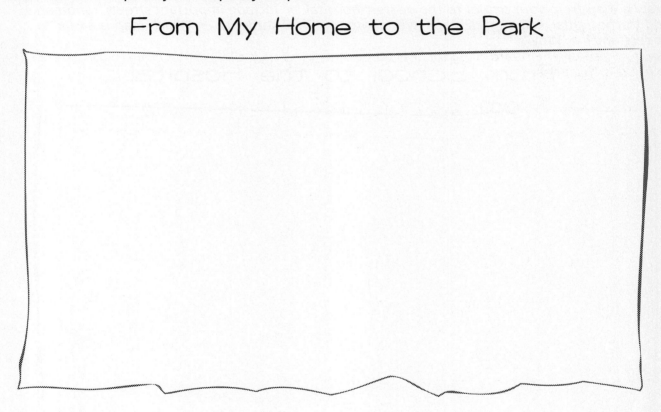

Class Project

How many different parks did your class write about? • *Make a list on the board of parks in your community.* • *Describe each park.* • *Plan a class trip to a park.* • *Have fun!*

Cross-Cultural Exchange

Tell the class about a special park in your country.

DIRECTIONS TO THE HOSPITAL

Find Someone Who . . .

Fill in the name of someone who

1. knows where the hospital is. _____

2. knows the name of the hospital. _____

3. has been to that hospital. _____

4. has had a good experience in the hospital. _____

5. has had a bad experience in the hospital. _____

Print with a Partner   Partner's Name _____

Draw a map from your school to the nearest hospital. • Include important streets, landmarks, and traffic lights. • Compare maps with another pair of students. • Which map is easier to understand? • Why?

From School to the Hospital

DRIVER LICENSE APPLICATION

Read with the Class

Read this application for a driver license with your class. • *Discuss any new vocabulary.*

Print

Fill in the driver license application on this page for yourself.

MV-44 (12/96)   **New York State Department of Motor Vehicles**

APPLICATION FOR DRIVER LICENSE "OR" NON-DRIVER ID CARD

*PLEASE **PRINT** IN BLUE OR BLACK INK IN THE WHITE BOXES*

Batch File No.

Image No.

LRC   LAM   LRN   LDP   LNO
LIS   LIN   POR   PAM   PRN   PDP

ARE YOU APPLYING FOR A? *(Check any that apply.)*

☐ Permit   ☐ ID card   ☐ Renewal   ☐ Duplicate   ☐ Change   ☐ Change out-of-state license for NYS license

VOTER REGISTRATION QUESTIONS *(Please answer "yes" or "no".)*

If you are not registered to vote where you live now, would you like to apply to register, or if you are changing your address, would you like the Board of Elections to be notified?

NOTE: If you do not check either box, you will be considered to have decided not to register to vote.

☐ *YES* - Complete Voter Registration Application Section

☐ *NO* - I Decline to Register/Already Registered/I do not want to notify the Board of Elections of my change of address.

LAST NAME   **FIRST NAME**   **MIDDLE NAME**

DATE OF BIRTH Month / Day / Year   **SEX** M ☐ F ☐   **HEIGHT**   **EYE COLOR**   **SOCIAL SECURITY NUMBER* (SSN)**

* All driver license applicants must supply their social security number. Authority to collect SSN is granted under Section 502 of the Vehicle and Traffic Law. The information will be used only for exchange with other jurisdictions and to invoke driver license sanctions for delinquent child/spouse support payments. Your number will not be given to the public or appear on any form or information request. Social security number is not required for Non-Driver ID applicants.

ADDRESS WHERE YOU GET YOUR MAIL *(Include Street Number and Name, Rural Delivery and/or Box Number)*   Apt. No.

CITY OR TOWN   **STATE**   **ZIP CODE**   **COUNTY**

ADDRESS WHERE YOU LIVE – *IF DIFFERENT FROM MAILING ADDRESS* – DO NOT GIVE P.O. BOX *(Include Street Number and Name, Rural Delivery, and/or Box Number)*   Apt. No.

CITY OR TOWN   **STATE**   **ZIP CODE**   **COUNTY**

Do you now have, or did you ever have: a New York driver license? ☐ YES ☐ NO   or a non-driver I.D. Card? ☐ YES ☐ NO

If "Yes", enter the identification number as it appears on the license or non-driver ID card.   **ID NUMBER**

ADDRESS CHANGE: CHECK BOX(ES): ☐ *MAILING ADDRESS*   ☐ *LEGAL ADDRESS*
Use form MV-232 (Address Change) if you have a vehicle registered in your name.

Does any of the information on your license or non-driver ID card need to be changed? ☐ YES ☐ NO

NAME CHANGE: *PRINT YOUR FORMER NAME EXACTLY AS IT APPEARS ON YOUR PRESENT LICENSE OR NON-DRIVER ID CARD.*

OTHER CHANGE: *WHAT IS THE CHANGE AND THE REASON FOR IT (new license class, wrong date of birth, etc.)?*

Do you have an out-of-state or Canadian license that is valid or that expired within the past year? ☐ YES ☐ NO

If "Yes", where was it issued: Date of Expiration:

Type of License   Driver License No.

Permission granted by New York State Department of Motor Vehicles

DRIVER LICENSE APPLICATION, p. 2

Group Survey

In groups of five, choose a recorder. • *Ask everyone these questions.* • *Record the answers.* • *Report your group answers to the class.*

1. How many students have a driver license in this state?
2. How many have a driver license in another state or in another country?
3. How many drive to school?
4. How many have a car?
5. How many want to apply for a driver license in this state?
6. How many will be organ donors?

GEOGRAPHIC REGIONS

Write with a Partner

Partner's Name ———————————————

With a partner, list everything you see in each of these regions. • Compare lists with another pair of students.

Group Brainstorm

In groups of three, discuss the scenes. • Then list answers to these questions. • Read your list to the class. • Then make a class list on the board.

1. What natural resources are in each region?
2. Which region probably has the largest population? Why?
3. What animals probably live in each region?
4. What work can people do in each region?
5. Which region would you like to visit? to live in? to read and know more about?

Partner Interview

Partner's Name ———————————————

Ask a partner these questions. • Write your partner's answers. • Read your answers to another pair of students.

1. What geographic region were you born in? What is special about it?
2. What geographic regions have you visited in your country?
3. What famous historical sites in your country have you visited?
4. What wild animals live in your region? Which ones have you seen?

Class Game: What Do You Remember?

Write the name of a place—a city, a state, a region, a tourist attraction—on a piece of paper. • Put the papers in a pile. • Choose one. • Read it to the class. • Name one natural resource or animal from that place.

VACATION POSTCARDS

Partner Interview

Partner's Name _____

Ask a partner these questions. • Write your partner's answers. • Read your partner's answers to another pair.

1. What did you do on your last vacation?
2. Where is a good place in your country for a vacation?
3. Tell me what is good about it.
4. Where would you like to take your "dream vacation?"

Write

Imagine you are enjoying your dream vacation. • Fill in this postcard. • Address it to your English class. • Read your postcard to the class.

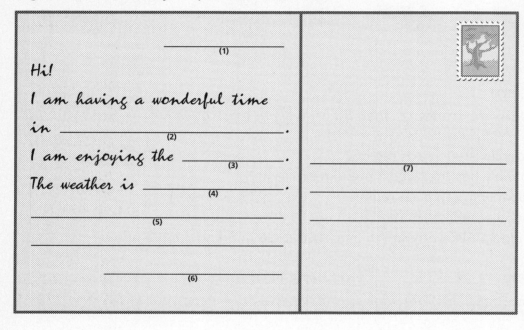

1. The date of your dream vacation

2. Choose one:
   • *Hawaii*
   • *Paris*
   • other:
   _____

3. Choose one:
   • *beach*
   • *trip*
   • *sights*
   • other:
   _____

4. Choose one:
   • *wonderful*
   • *perfect*
   • other:
   _____

5. Choose one:
   • *I'd like to stay here forever!*
   • *The week has flown by!*
   • other:
   _____

6. Your name

7. The name and address of your class

Read with the Class

Bring vacation postcards to class. • Explain where the postcards are from.

LETTERS ABOUT A VISIT

Partner Interview

Partner's Name _____

Ask a partner these questions. • *Write your partner's answers.* • *Read your partner's answers to another pair.*

1. Do you ever visit friends or relatives?
2. Which friends or relatives do you visit?
3. Where do they live?
4. What do you do there?
5. How often do you visit them?

Write with a Partner

With your class, add more choices. • *Then complete this letter to the same partner.* • *Imagine that your partner will visit you in your country or in another favorite place during the best time of the year.* • *Exchange letters with your partner.* • *Read your partner's letter.*

_____ (1)

Dear _____ (2) ,

   I'm so glad you can come for a visit. Let me know when you will be arriving. The weather should be _____ (3) . Bring _____ (4) and _____ (4) with you so we can

_____ (5) .

   I am really looking forward to seeing you again.

_____ (6) ,

_____ (7)

1. Today's date
2. Your partner's name
3. Choose one:
   • *rainy*
   • *hot*
   • *snowy*
   • other: _____
4. Choose two:
   • *warm clothes*
   • *a bathing suit*
   • *boots*
   • other: _____
5. Choose one:
   • *go to the beach*
   • *go skiing*
   • *go sightseeing*
   • other: _____
6. Choose one
   • *Love*
   • *Always*
   • *Until then*
7. Your signature

LETTERS ABOUT A VISIT, p. 2

Write with a Partner

Complete this answer to your partner's letter.

_____ (1)

Dear _____ (2) ,

    Thanks for your letter. It will be good to see you again and to be in _____ (3) in the _____ (4) . I will be sure to bring _____ (5) and _____ (5) so that we can _____ (6) . I'll be arriving on _____ (7) Flight 758 at 8:30 p.m. on _____ (8) _____. See you then.

_____ (9) ,

_____ (10)

1. Today's date
2. Your partner's name
3. Your partner's country or favorite place
4. Choose one:
   - *spring*
   - *summer*
   - *autumn*
   - *winter*
5. The clothing from your partner's letter
6. The activity from your partner's letter
7. Name of an airline company
8. Ask your partner for the best date, and write it.
9. Choose one:
   - *Love*
   - *Until then*
   - other:

   _____

10. Your signature

CUSTOMS DECLARATION

Cross-Cultural Exchange

Did anyone in your class ever fill out a Customs Declaration? • Where? When? • In what language? • Tell the class about it?

Partner Interview

Partner's Name _____

Imagine you are going on a trip to the U.S. • Tell a partner about the trip. • Ask these questions about your partner's trip. • Write your partner's answers in the Activities section of your notebook. • Tell the class about your partner's trip.

1. What airline are you using?
2. Who is going with you?
3. Where are you going?
4. How long are you staying?

5. What is the purpose of your trip?
6. How much money are you taking with you?
7. What other things are you taking with you?

Print with the Class

Fill in this Customs Declaration. • Use the information from your Partner Interview.

WELCOME TO THE UNITED STATES

DEPARTMENT OF THE TREASURY
UNITED STATES CUSTOMS SERVICE

FORM APPROVED
OMB NO. 1515-0041

CUSTOMS DECLARATION

Each arriving traveler or head of family must provide the following information (only **ONE** written declaration per family is required):

1. Name: ....
   Last   First   Middle Initial

2. Date of Birth: ...../...../..... 3. Airline/Flight ....
   Day Month Year

4. Number of family members traveling with you.....................

5. U.S. Address: ....
   City: .... State: ....

6. I am a U.S. Citizen   YES ☐   NO ☐
   If No,
   Country: ....

7. I reside permanently in the U.S.   YES ☐   NO ☐
   If No,
   Expected Length of Stay: ....

8. The purpose of my trip is or was ☐ BUSINESS ☐ PLEASURE

9. I am/we are bringing fruits, plants, meats, food,   YES ☐   NO ☐
   soil, birds, snails, other live animals, farm
   products, or I/we have been on a farm or ranch
   outside the U.S.

10. I am/we are carrying currency or monetary   YES ☐   NO ☐
    instruments over $10,000 U.S. or foreign
    equivalent.

11. The total value of all goods I/we purchased or
    acquired abroad and am/are bringing to the U.S.
    is (see instructions under Merchandise on reverse
    side): $ ....
                                                US Dollars

WARNING

The smuggling or unlawful importation of controlled substances regardless of amount is a violation of U.S. law.

Accuracy of your declaration may be verified through questioning and physical search.

AGRICULTURAL PRODUCTS

To prevent the entry of dangerous agricultural pests the following are restricted: Fruits, vegetables, plants, plant products, soil, meats, meat products, birds, snails, and other live animals or animal products. Failure to declare all such items to a Customs/Agriculture Officer can result in fines or other penalties.

CURRENCY AND MONETARY INSTRUMENTS

The transportation of currency or monetary instruments, regardless of amount, is legal; however, if you take out of or bring into (or are about to take out of or bring into) the United States more than $10,000 (U.S. or foreign equivalent, or a combination of the two) in coin, currency, travelers checks or bearer instruments such as money orders, checks, stocks or bonds, you are required by law to file a report on a Form 4790 with the U.S. Customs Service. If you have someone else carry the currency or instruments for you, you must also file the report. FAILURE TO FILE THE REQUIRED REPORT OR FALSE STATEMENTS ON THE REPORT MAY LEAD TO SEIZURE OF THE CURRENCY OR INSTRUMENTS AND TO CIVIL PENALTIES AND/OR CRIMINAL PROSECUTION.

MERCHANDISE

In Item 11, **U.S. residents** must declare the total value of ALL articles acquired abroad (whether new or used, whether dutiable or not, and whether obtained by purchase, as a gift, or otherwise), including those purchases made in DUTY FREE stores in the U.S. or abroad, which are in their or their family's possession at the time of arrival. **Visitors** must declare in Item 11 the total value of all gifts and commercial items, including samples they are bringing with them.

The amount of duty to be paid will be determined by a Customs officer. U.S. residents are normally entitled to a duty free exemption of $400 on those items accompanying them; non-residents are normally entitled to an exemption of $100. Both residents and non-residents will normally be required to pay a flat 10% rate of duty on the first $1,000 above their exemptions.

If the value of goods declared in Item 11 EXCEEDS $1,400 PER PERSON, then list ALL articles below and show price paid *in U.S. dollars* or, for gifts, fair retail value. If additional space is needed, continue on another Customs Form 6059B.

DESCRIPTION OF ARTICLES	PRICE	CUSTOMS USE
TOTAL		

IF YOU HAVE ANY QUESTIONS ABOUT WHAT MUST BE REPORTED OR DECLARED ASK A CUSTOMS OFFICER.

I have read the above statements and have made a truthful declaration.

SIGNATURE — DATE (Day/Month/Year)

*U.S.G.P.O. 1990-744-875   Customs Form 6059B (092089) (Back)

Write with a Partner   Partner's Name _____

With a partner, write a conversation with a U.S. Customs Inspector. • Ask and answer questions about the Customs Declaration. • Read your conversation to the class.

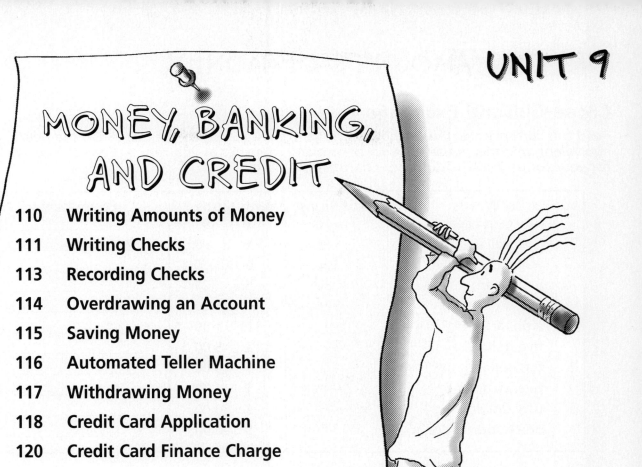

UNIT 9

MONEY, BANKING, AND CREDIT

SPELLING HINT

➤ The **long i sound** is usually spelled **i (consonant) e**, or **ie**, or just **y**.

t**i**m**e**	p**ie**	m**y**
dr**i**v**e**	l**ie**	tr**y**
inv**i**t**e**	d**ie**	fl**y**

WRITING AMOUNTS OF MONEY

Cross-Cultural Exchange

Read this currency chart. • *It shows ways to express money in the U.S.* • *On the board, list equivalent amounts in the currency of as many countries as you can.* • *Copy the equivalents for your country on the Currency Chart below.*

In Words	With Signs	With Signs	Equivalents
one cent (penny)	1¢	$ .01	_____
a nickel	5¢	$ .05	_____
a dime	10¢	$ .10	_____
a quarter	25¢	$ .25	_____
a half dollar	50¢	$ .50	_____
a dollar	—	$ 1.00	_____
five dollars	—	$ 5.00	_____
ten dollars	—	$ 10.00	_____
twenty dollars	—	$ 20.00	_____
fifty dollars	—	$ 50.00	_____
one hundred dollars	—	$ 100.00	_____

Write with a Partner

Partner's Name _____

Write these amounts using numerals. • *Compare your answers with another pair of students.*

1. one dollar and ninety-nine cents $1.99
2. one dollar and sixty-seven cents   _____
3. a dollar and a half   _____
4. two dollars and twenty-five cents   _____

5. ten dollars and two cents   _____
6. fifteen dollars and fifty cents   _____
7. ninety dollars and nineteen cents   _____
8. five cents   _____

Write with a Group

In groups of four, read the amounts of money below. • *Then write the amounts by using words.*

1. $2.45 _____
2. $10.95 _____
3. $49.99 _____
4. $186.00 _____

Listen and Write

Partner's Name _____

Dictate five amounts of money to a partner. • *Then write as your partner dictates to you.* • *Exchange papers and mark any corrections needed.* • *Then return your partner's paper.*

WRITING CHECKS

Class Brainstorm

List on the board places in your community that accept checks as payment for bills.

Write

On the memo line, write what this check is for. • *Then sign your name.*

Continue Writing

With your class, add more choices. • *Then write this check to pay a bill.*

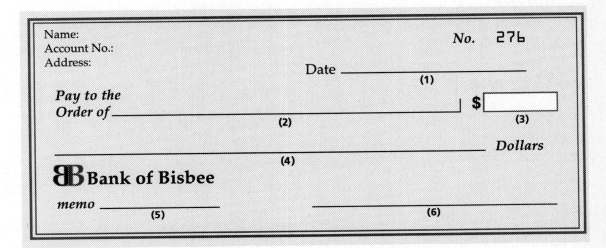

1. Today's date
2. Choose one:
   • name of the
     electric company
   • name of the
     gas company
   • name of the
     phone company
   • other:

   _____

3. The check amount in numerals
4. The check amount in words
5. Choose one:
   • *electric bill*
   • *gas bill*
   • *phone bill*
   • other:

   _____

6. Your signature

WRITING CHECKS, p.2

Write with a Partner

Partner's Name _____

With your partner add more choices. • *Write this check to your partner.* • *Show the check to your partner and explain it.*

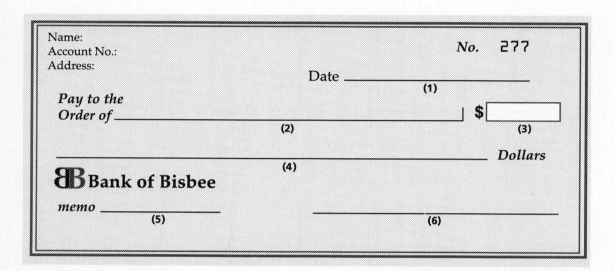

1. Today's date
2. Your partner's name
3. The check amount in numerals
4. The check amount in words
5. Choose one:
   • *gift*
   • *loan*
   • *repay loan*
   • other:

   _____

6. Your signature

RECORDING CHECKS

Read with a Group

In groups of three or four, read this checkbook receipt page and answer the questions below. • Compare your answers with the class.

1. What was the balance in the account before June 4th? _____

2. What was the June 4th check issued to? _____

3. How much was the check for? _____

4. How much money was deposited into the checking account on June 6th? _____

		PLEASE BE SURE TO DEDUCT ANY PER CHECK CHARGES OR SERVICE CHARGES THAT MAY APPLY TO YOUR ACCOUNT					BALANCE	
CHECK NO	DATE	CHECKS ISSUED TO OR DESCRIPTION OF DEPOSIT	(-) AMOUNT OF CHECK		(-) CHECK FEE	AMOUNT OF DEPOSIT	223	00
278	6/4	Marie's Gift Shop	17	50			17	50
						BAL	205	50
	6/6	Deposit				63 00	63	–
						BAL	268	50
						BAL		

Write

Write this check to pay Dr. Katz $154.25 for dental work. • Record this check on the receipt page above. • Subtract this check from the balance. • What is the new balance?

Name:
Account No.:
Address:

No. 279

Date _____

Pay to the
Order of _____ $ [____]

_____ Dollars

BB Bank of Bisbee

memo _____

OVERDRAWING AN ACCOUNT

Write

With your class, add more choices. • Write this check to a store where you like to shop. • Record the check on the checkbook receipt page below.

```
┌─────────────────────────────────────────────────────────────────┐
│  Name:                                                            │
│  Account No.:                              No.    280             │
│  Address:                                                         │
│                               Date _____    │
│   Pay to the                              (1)                     │
│   Order of _____  $ ┌──────────────┐    │
│                        (2)                     │              │    │
│                                                └──────────────┘    │
│   _____  Dollars  (3) │
│                            (4)                                    │
│   ℬℬ Bank of Bisbee                                               │
│                                                                   │
│   memo _____        _____  │
│                (5)                          (6)                   │
└─────────────────────────────────────────────────────────────────┘
```

1. Today's date
2. Name of store
3. $131.95
4. $131.95 in words

5. Choose one:
   • *clothes*
   • *TV set*
   • *car equipment*
   • other: _____
6. Your signature

Write with a Group

In groups of four, subtract this check amount from the balance on this checkbook receipt page. • Discuss these questions. • Report your group's answers to the class.

1. What is the balance?
2. What is the problem?

3. What will the bank do next?
4. What can the person do?

PLEASE BE SURE TO DEDUCT ANY PER CHECK CHARGES OR SERVICE CHARGES THAT MAY APPLY TO YOUR ACCOUNT

CHECK NO	DATE	CHECKS ISSUED TO OR DESCRIPTION OF DEPOSIT	(-) AMOUNT OF CHECK		(-) CHECK FEE	AMOUNT OF DEPOSIT		BALANCE	
								223	00
278	6/4	Marie's Gift Shop	17	50				17	50
							BAL	205	50
	6/6	Deposit				63	00	63	—
							BAL	268	50
279	6/10	Dr. Katz	154	25				154	25
							BAL	114	25
							BAL		

SAVING MONEY

Find Someone Who. . .

Fill in the name of someone who

1. saves money in a bank. _____

2. saves money in a secret place. _____

3. can't save money. _____

4. likes to save money. _____

5. saves money every month. _____

6. doesn't like to save money. _____

Write

Fill out this deposit ticket to deposit a check for $125.63 and $50.00 cash in your savings account. • *What is your net deposit?*

		SAVINGS DEPOSIT	
	LIST CHECKS BY BANK NO.	DOLLARS	CENTS
ACCOUNT NUMBER _____	CURRENCY		
NAME (PLEASE PRINT) _____	COIN		
ADDRESS _____	CHECKS		
CITY STATE ZIP CODE	TOTAL OF CHECKS LISTED ON REVERSE		
PLEASE SIGN IN TELLER'S PRESENCE FOR CASH RECEIVED	SUBTOTAL		
QB Oceanside Bank	◄LESS CASH RECEIVED		
:04112300998: DATE	NET DEPOSIT $ _____		

Cross-Cultural Exchange

In groups of four, answer these questions. • *Report your group's answers to the class.*

1. How do people save money in your country?
2. What do people save money for in your country?
3. Is it easier or harder to save money where you live now?
4. What are the advantages and disadvantages of saving money in a bank?

AUTOMATED TELLER MACHINE

Class Survey

Survey the class. • Ask these questions. • Discuss the answers.

1. *How many students know what an ATM is?* _____

2. *How many students have an ATM card?* _____

3. *How many students have used an ATM to withdraw cash?* _____

4. *How many students have used an ATM for a deposit?* _____

5. *How many students have used an ATM to make a payment?* _____

Print

Fill in this deposit envelope to deposit a check for $64.27 at an ATM.

Deposit/Payment Envelope

Please include a deposit slip or payment coupon

BB Bank of Bisbee

Name _____

Account Number _____

Daytime Phone Number _____

☐ Checking deposit   Amount $ _____
☐ Savings deposit
☐ Payment

Availability of Deposits
Funds from deposits may not be available for immediate withdrawal. You will be notified if a hold has been placed on any deposited funds. If you have a question about this, a branch representative can help you.

ATM-ENV   **All transactions are subject to final proof and verification.**

Write

Before you deposit the check, you must endorse it (sign your name on the back of the check). • Endorse this check.

ENDORSE HERE

X
....

DO NOT WRITE, STAMP, OR SIGN BELOW THIS LINE
⬧ RESERVED FOR FINANCIAL INSTITUTION USE ⬧

116

WITHDRAWING MONEY

Group Brainstorm

In groups of four, list good reasons to withdraw money from savings. • Read your list to the class.

Write

Fill out this Withdrawal Voucher to withdraw one hundred dollars from your savings account.

WITHDRAWAL For Use in Banking Room Only Pass Book No. ....

Received from **FIRST BANK**

.... **Dollars**

	Dollars	Cents
Sign Here..	$	

Address...

Check # .... Payable to: ....

Name:
Account No.:
Address:

No. 281

Date _____
(1)

*Pay to the
Order of* _____ $ [_____]
(2) (3)

_____ *Dollars*
(4)

BB Bank of Bisbee

memo _____ _____
(5) (6)

Write

Write this check to withdraw money from your checking account. • Endorse it on the back.

1. Today's date
2. *Cash*
3. Any amount of money
4. Same amount of money in words
5. Purpose of check
6. Your signature

ENDORSE HERE

X _____

CREDIT CARD APPLICATION

Class Survey

Survey your class. • *Ask these questions.* • *Discuss the results of the survey.*

1. How many students use credit cards? _____

2. How many have a "universal" credit card? _____

3. How many have a store credit card? _____

4. How many have a gas credit card? _____

5. How many don't like credit cards? Why? _____

Read with Your Class

Read this credit card application with your class.

Credit Card Application

IMPORTANT: PLEASE PRINT USING CAPITAL LETTERS AND COMPLETE ALL INFORMATION.

FIRST, MIDDLE, LAST NAME (LEAVE SPACE BETWEEN EACH) | DATE OF BIRTH - (MO. DAY YR.)

HOME ADDRESS | APT. NO. | CITY | STATE | ZIP CODE

HOME TELEPHONE ( ) | BUSINESS TELEPHONE ( ) | SOCIAL SECURITY NUMBER | NO. OF DEPENDENTS (EXCLUDING YOURSELF)

ARE YOU A U.S. CITIZEN? ☐ YES ☐ NO (EXPLAIN IMMIGRATION STATUS) | ARE YOU A PERMANENT U.S. RESIDENT? ☐ YES ☐ NO | DO YOU? ☐ OWN ☐ LIVE WITH PARENTS ☐ RENT ☐ OTHER (EXPLAIN) | MONTHLY RENT OR MORTGAGE $ | MOTHER'S MAIDEN NAME

ABOUT YOUR JOB & FINANCES

EMPLOYER/UNIVERSITY OR COLLEGE | ADDRESS | CITY | STATE | ZIP CODE

HOW LONG? YEARS MONTHS | OCCUPATION | YEARLY GROSS SALARY $ | OTHER INCOME* $ ☐ PER MONTH ☐ PER YEAR | SOURCE OF OTHER INCOME | DO YOU HAVE A ☐ CHECKING ACCOUNT ☐ SAVINGS ACCOUNT | ARE YOU ☐ SELF-EMPLOYED ☐ RETIRED ☐ STUDENT

*Alimony, child support or separate maintenance income need not be disclosed if you do not wish to have it considered as a basis for paying this obligation.

ABOUT YOUR CO-APPLICANT Complete if you are relying on the income of another person to qualify for an account.

FIRST, MIDDLE, LAST NAME (LEAVE SPACE BETWEEN EACH)

DATE OF BIRTH (MO. DAY YR.) | HOME TELEPHONE ( ) | BUSINESS TELEPHONE ( ) | SOCIAL SECURITY NUMBER

RELATIONSHIP TO APPLICANT: ☐ SPOUSE ☐ OTHER (EXPLAIN) | HOME ADDRESS (IF DIFFERENT FROM ADDRESS ABOVE) | CITY | STATE | ZIP CODE

EMPLOYER/UNIVERSITY OR COLLEGE | ADDRESS | CITY | STATE | ZIP CODE

YEARLY GROSS SALARY $ | OTHER INCOME* $ ☐ PER MONTH ☐ PER YEAR | SOURCE OF OTHER INCOME

*Alimony, child support or separate maintenance income need not be disclosed if you do not wish to have it considered as a basis for paying this obligation.

CREDIT CARD APPLICATION, p. 2

Print

Fill in this credit card application.

Credit Card Application

IMPORTANT: PLEASE PRINT USING CAPITAL LETTERS AND COMPLETE ALL INFORMATION.

FIRST, MIDDLE, LAST NAME (LEAVE SPACE BETWEEN EACH) | DATE OF BIRTH - (MO. DAY YR.)

HOME ADDRESS | APT. NO. | CITY | STATE | ZIP CODE

HOME TELEPHONE (   ) | BUSINESS TELEPHONE (   ) | SOCIAL SECURITY NUMBER | NO. OF DEPENDENTS (EXCLUDING YOURSELF)

ARE YOU A U.S. CITIZEN? ☐ YES ☐ NO (EXPLAIN IMMIGRATION STATUS) | ARE YOU A PERMANENT U.S. RESIDENT? ☐ YES ☐ NO | DO YOU? ☐ OWN ☐ LIVE WITH PARENTS ☐ RENT ☐ OTHER (EXPLAIN) | MONTHLY RENT OR MORTGAGE $ | MOTHER'S MAIDEN NAME

ABOUT YOUR JOB & FINANCES

EMPLOYER/UNIVERSITY OR COLLEGE | ADDRESS | CITY | STATE | ZIP CODE

HOW LONG? YEARS   MONTHS | OCCUPATION | YEARLY GROSS SALARY $ | OTHER INCOME* $ ☐ PER MONTH ☐ PER YEAR | SOURCE OF OTHER INCOME | DO YOU HAVE A ☐ CHECKING ACCOUNT ☐ SAVINGS ACCOUNT | ARE YOU ☐ SELF-EMPLOYED ☐ RETIRED ☐ STUDENT

*Alimony, child support or separate maintenance income need not be disclosed if you do not wish to have it considered as a basis for paying this obligation.

ABOUT YOUR CO-APPLICANT Complete if you are relying on the income of another person to qualify for an account.

FIRST, MIDDLE, LAST NAME (LEAVE SPACE BETWEEN EACH)

DATE OF BIRTH (MO. DAY YR.) | HOME TELEPHONE (   ) | BUSINESS TELEPHONE (   ) | SOCIAL SECURITY NUMBER

RELATIONSHIP TO APPLICANT: ☐ SPOUSE ☐ OTHER (EXPLAIN) | HOME ADDRESS (IF DIFFERENT FROM ADDRESS ABOVE) | CITY | STATE | ZIP CODE

EMPLOYER/UNIVERSITY OR COLLEGE | ADDRESS | CITY | STATE | ZIP CODE

YEARLY GROSS SALARY $ | OTHER INCOME* $ ☐ PER MONTH ☐ PER YEAR | SOURCE OF OTHER INCOME

*Alimony, child support or separate maintenance income need not be disclosed if you do not wish to have it considered as a basis for paying this obligation.

PLEASE SIGN BELOW

I authorize Brettwood Trust Company to check my credit record and to verify my credit, employment and income references. I agree that if I use my Card or Account I will be subject to the terms and charges specified in the Brettwood Cardmember agreement which has been sent with my card. I certify that I am age 18 or older and that the information provided is accurate. I understand the information contained in this application may be shared with Brettwood Trust Company's corporate affiliates.

X _____   X _____
Signature   Date   Co-Applicant   Date

OPTIONAL CREDITSAFE® PLUS INSURANCE PLAN

YES, please enroll me in the optional CreditSafe® Plus credit insurance plan. I have read and understand the insurance and cost disclosures and I meet the eligibility requirements listed. I understand that the monthly premium will be billed to my account and that I am free to cancel at any time.   X _____

Group Brainstorm

In groups of four, choose a recorder. • List places in your community where credit cards are accepted. • Read your list to the class. • Make a class list on the board.

CREDIT CARD FINANCE CHARGE

Read with Your Class

Read this credit card monthly statement. • *Answer these questions about the statement.*

ACCOUNT NUMBER	47-002-828-274	PREVIOUS BALANCE	114.00	Telephoning about billing errors will not preserve your rights under federal law. To preserve your rights, please write to the address in Section 7 on the back.
ACCOUNT TYPE	FLEX	TOTAL PURCHASES & CHARGES	203.43	
PAYMENT DUE DATE	12/30/98	TOTAL CREDITS	.00	NOTICE: SEE REVERSE SIDE FOR IMPORTANT INFORMATION.
BILL CLOSING DATE	12/05/98	TOTAL PAYMENTS	.00	FOR CREDIT CARD ACCOUNT INFORMATION CALL: 1-800-555-6029
		FINANCE CHARGE	3.61	

```
   DATE _____    RECORD
                         YOUR
AMOUNT PAID _____   PAYMENT
                         DETAILS
   CHECK # _____   HERE
```

THIS IS YOUR NEW BALANCE	321.04
MINIMUM PAYMENT NOW DUE	38.00

PERIODIC RATE	ANNUAL PERCENTAGE RATE	BALANCE SUBJECT TO FINANCE CHARGE	BALANCE METHOD	
.05918% DAILY	21.60	115.28	B	THE CREDITOR UNDER THIS ACCOUNT IS FD NATIONAL BANK

1. What was the previous balance?
2. How much was paid last month?
3. How much was charged last month?
4. How much is owed now?
5. What is the minimum payment now?
6. What is the finance charge for last month?
7. What is the annual percentage rate for this credit card?
8. How can more finance charges be avoided?

Write with a Partner   Partner's Name _____

With a partner, decide how much to pay on this credit card balance. • *Fill in the check to make your payment.* • *Compare your checks with another pair of students.* • *Explain why you chose to pay that amount.*

```
Name:
Account No.:                              No.  282
Address:
                         Date _____

Pay to the
Order of _____  | $ _____

_____   Dollars

BB Bank of Bisbee

memo _____    _____
```

EMPLOYMENT

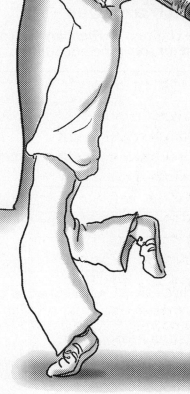

SPELLING HINT

➤ The **long o sound** is usually spelled **ow**, **oa**, or just **o**.

own	t**oa**st	n**o**
sh**ow**	r**oa**st	hell**o**
wind**ow**	b**oa**st	s**o**da

COVER LETTER

Read with a Group

In groups of four, read these Help Wanted ads. • Discuss the vocabulary. • Decide on jobs to apply for. • Tell another group about your choices.

EMPLOYMENT OPPORTUNITIES

ADVERTISING – Fast-paced design firm seeks versatile A.D. w/ expert Mac skills. Min. 5yrs. exp. Copywriting and/or Multimedia capabilities. Send résumé to: Ali Sharif, 1214 Brown Street, Mountain Lake, NY 10533

ASST. MGR.
GRAND OPENING
Mohawk based electronic book & business supply co. is opening a new location. Need people to learn all areas, must be good w/ cust & co-workers. Send résumé and cover letter to 12 Oak Street, Hohokus, NJ 07413   Attn: Robyn Banino

CARPENTER – Resid/comm'l.   Must have tools and transp. w/ at least 3 yrs exp. Call Larry Peralta btwn 9am- 5pm 221-555-7942

CLERK/RECEPTIONIST ENTRY LEVEL Full or P/T. Must be bilingual. Entry level position, will train. Exc oppty for ambitious person. Fax résumé to 201-555-3209 attn: Manager

Write with a Group

Add more choices. • Then write a cover letter for one of the jobs. • Exchange letters in the group. • Edit someone else's letter. • Discuss the changes you made.

_____ (1)

_____ (2)

_____ (3)

_____ (4)

Dear _____ (5),

I would like to apply for the position of _____ (6) _____ I saw advertised in the Star Daily News.

As I hope you will see from my enclosed résumé, I have had good experience for this job. I can come in for an interview any morning.

Thank you for considering me for this position.

Sincerely,

_____ (7)

_____ (8)

1. Your address
2. The date
3. Name of person to contact (See ad)
4. Address (in ad)
5. Choose one:
   • Sir
   • Madam
   • Mr./Mrs./Ms.

   _____

   (See ad)
   • other:

   _____

6. The job you are applying for
7. Sign your name
8. Type or print your name

Write with a Partner

Partner's Name _____

With a partner, write a telephone conversation as a follow up to your cover letter and résumé. • Ask for an interview. • Read your conversation to another pair of students.

RÉSUMÉ

Read with the Class

Study this résumé together. • *Discuss the vocabulary.* • *What does a résumé include?*

Raoul Martínez
2914 Jerome Avenue
Bronx, New York 10468
(718) 365-8758

SKILLS

- Organizing and supervising inventory control
- Operating and maintaining stitching equipment, large trucks
- Bilingual in Spanish and English

EDUCATION

1996 **Associate of Arts**
NORTH CENTRAL COMMUNITY COLLEGE, Brooklyn, New York

1993 **High School General Equivalency Diploma**
COMMUNITY CENTER, Bronx, New York

WORK EXPERIENCE

1995 – present INTERNATIONAL SHOE MACHINERY COMPANY, Yonkers, New York
Foreman
- Supervise eight workers in supply department
- Track and maintain inventory for various departments

1993 – 1995 UNION SHOE FACTORY, Albany, New York
Team Leader, Stitching Department (1994–1995)
- Supervised three stitchers on the assembly line
Stitcher, Assembly Line (1993)

1990 – 1993 UNITED TRUCKING COMPANY, Princeton, New Jersey
Truck Driver
- Maintained and drove Mack truck (piggyback)
- Delivered cargo throughout eastern United States

REFERENCES

Available upon request

RÉSUMÉ, p. 2

Write

Follow the model résumé. • *Write your résumé.*

_____
(name)

_____
(your street address)

_____
(your city, state, and ZIP code)

_____
(your area code and telephone number)

SKILLS
(optional)

• _____

• _____

• _____

EDUCATION

_____
(year)

_____
(full name of certificate or degree)

_____
(name of school)   (location)

_____
(year)

_____

_____

EXPERIENCE

_____ - _____
(from)   (to)

_____
(name of company)   (location)

_____
(position)

• _____
(responsibilities, accomplishments)

• _____

• _____

_____ - _____
(from)   (to)

_____
(name of company)   (location)

_____
(position)

• _____
(responsibilities, accomplishments)

• _____

• _____

Write with a Partner   Partner's Name _____

Show your résumé to a partner. • *Explain your résumé.* • *With your partner, write five questions to ask about your education and job experience.* • *Ask and answer the questions.*

EMPLOYMENT APPLICATION

Read with the Class

Study this application. • Discuss the vocabulary. • What does an employment application include?

Write

Use the information from your résumé to fill in the information on this application.

PERSONAL DATA

Name: Last: _____ First: _____ Middle: _____

Current Address: Street and Number: _____

City _____ State _____ Zip _____

Preferred Name or Nickname: _____

Day Phone Number: (   )_____ Evening Phone Number: (   )_____

How or by whom were you referred? _____

Position Desired: 1)_____ 2) _____

Social Security No. _____

Have you applied here before? ☐ Yes ☐ No   If yes, give dates: _____

If hired and under 18, can you furnish a work permit? ☐ Yes ☐ No ☐ I am over 18

If applicable: Military Service Status: ☐ Active ☐ Inactive   Branch:_____

Are you legally authorized to work in the United States? ☐ Yes ☐ No
(If hired, you will be required to submit proof of your identity and legal work authorization as a condition of employment.)

Do you have any relatives employed at this company? ☐ Yes ☐ No

If yes, give name and location employed: _____

Have you ever been employed by this company? ☐ Yes ☐ No

If yes, give dates and location employed: _____

Do you have specific salary requirements? ☐ Yes ☐ No   If yes, please indicate: _____

EMPLOYMENT DATA

Date Available for work:_____ Total hours available per week: _____

Type of hours: ☐ Full Time ☐ Part Time ☐ Days* ☐ Nights* *Hours:_____

☐ Regular ☐ Temporary/What date will you no longer be available for work? _____

Will you work overtime if necessary? ☐ Yes ☐ No   If yes, how many hours per week? _____

Are there any days or hours you are unable or unwilling to work? If yes, write specifics below:

_____

Do you have transportation to/from work? ☐ Yes ☐ No

What is the most amount of time you wish to spend commuting to work? _____

Will you travel? ☐ Yes ☐ No   If yes, what percent of your time? (where) _____

Are you willing to relocate? ☐ Yes ☐ No If yes, where? _____

AN EQUAL OPPORTUNITY/DRUG-FREE EMPLOYER

We are an equal opportunity employer and do not discriminate against any applicant because of race, color, religion, sex, national origin, age, disability, sexual orientation, marital status, veteran status, or any other legally protected group.

EMPLOYMENT APPLICATION, p. 2

REFERENCES

Name: _____ Date _____

Position Applied for: _____ Location: _____

Professional References

Please list 3 professional references who can verify your work history and performance. References should not be relatives and at least two must have directly supervised you at some time in your work history.

Please print:

1. **Name of Supervisor** _____ Title _____
   Company Name and Address _____
   Company Phone Number including area code and extension _____

2. **Name of Supervisor** _____ Title _____
   Company Name and Address _____
   Company Phone Number including area code and extension _____

3. **Name of Supervisor** _____ Title _____
   Company Name and Address _____
   Company Phone Number including area code and extension _____

Personal References

Please list 2 personal references (must not be a relative).

1. Name and Address _____
   Phone Number including area code and extension _____
   Occupation _____
   Years Acquainted: _____
   How do you know this individual? _____

2. Name and Address _____
   Phone Number including area code and extension _____
   Occupation _____
   Years Acquainted: _____
   How do you know this individual? _____

Read with a Partner   Partner's Name _____

Read a partner's employment application. • Ask questions about the information.

SOCIAL SECURITY CARD

Read with a Group

In groups of four, look at this card. • *Answer the questions.*

1. What is the social security number?
2. Who does the card belong to?
3. Do you have a social security number? Write the number:

   _____

4. What should you do if you lose your social security card?

   _____

   _____

Contact any social security office immediately if you:
▶ lose your card—to get a duplicate card.
▶ change your name—to get a card in your new name.
▶ are unable to work because of a severe disability expected to last a year or more.
▶ are 62 or older—to ask about retirement checks.
▶ are within 2 or 3 months of age 65, even if you don't plan to retire—to sign up for Medicare.

U.S. Department of Health, Education, and Welfare
Social Security Administration
Form OA-702 Rev. (1-72)

Class Brainstorm

Make a list on the board of uses for a social security number.

Community Activity

Use a telephone book. • *Look under United States Government.* • *Look up the address and phone number of the nearest Social Security Office.* • *Write the information.*

_____

_____

_____

Write with a Partner   Partner's Name _____

With a partner, write a telephone conversation requesting an application for a social security card. • *Read your conversation to another pair of students.*

EMPLOYEE'S WITHHOLDING ALLOWANCE CERTIFICATE (W-4)

Read with the Class

Study this **Personal Allowances Worksheet** and **Employee's Withholding Allowance Certificate** with your class. • Discuss the vocabulary. • What allowances are there? • Who can claim exemption from withholding?

Write

Fill in the information for yourself.

Personal Allowances Worksheet

A Enter "1" for **yourself** if no one else can claim you as a dependent . . . . **A** _____

B Enter "1" if:
- You are single and have only one job; or
- You are married, have only one job, and your spouse does not work; or } . . **B** _____
- Your wages from a second job or your spouse's wages (or the total of both) are $1,000 or less.

C Enter "1" for your **spouse.** But, you may choose to enter -0- if you are married and have either a working spouse or more than one job. (This may help you avoid having too little tax withheld.). . . . . **C** _____

D Enter number of **dependents** (other than your spouse or yourself) you will claim on your tax return . . . . **D** _____

E Enter "1" if you will file as **head of household** on your tax return (see conditions under **Head of household** above) . **E** _____

F Enter "1" if you have at least $1,500 of **child or dependent care expenses** for which you plan to claim a credit . . **F** _____

G **New—Child Tax Credit:** • If your total income will be between $16,500 and $47,000 ($21,000 and $60,000 if married), enter "1" for each eligible child. • If your total income will be between $47,000 and $80,000 ($60,000 and $115,000 if married), enter "1" if you have two or three eligible children, or enter "2" if you have four or more . . . . **G** _____

H Add lines A through G and enter total here. **Note:** This amount may be different from the number of exemptions you claim on your return. ▶ **H** _____

For accuracy, complete all worksheets that apply.	• If you plan to **itemize or claim adjustments to income** and want to reduce your withholding, see the Deductions and Adjustments Worksheet on page 2. • If you are **single,** have **more than one job,** and your combined earnings from all jobs exceed $32,000 OR if you are **married** and have a **working spouse or more than one job,** and the combined earnings from all jobs exceed $55,000, see the Two-Earner/Two-Job Worksheet on page 2 to avoid having too little tax withheld. • If **neither** of the above situations applies, **stop here** and enter the number from line H on line 5 of Form W-4 below.

- - - - - - - - - - - - **Cut here and give the certificate to your employer. Keep the top part for your records.** - - - - - - - - - - - -

Form **W-4** Department of the Treasury Internal Revenue Service	**Employee's Withholding Allowance Certificate** ▶ **For Privacy Act and Paperwork Reduction Act Notice, see page 2.**	OMB No. 1545-0010 **1998**

1 Type or print your first name and middle initial	Last name	**2** Your social security number

Home address (number and street or rural route)	**3** ☐ Single ☐ Married ☐ Married, but withhold at higher Single rate. **Note:** If married, but legally separated, or spouse is a nonresident alien, check the Single box.
City or town, state, and ZIP code	**4** If your last name differs from that on your social security card, check here and call 1-800-772-1213 for a new card . . . . ▶ ☐

5 Total number of allowances you are claiming (from line H above or from the worksheets on page 2 if they apply) . | **5** _____

6 Additional amount, if any, you want withheld from each paycheck . . . . | **6** $ _____

7 I claim exemption from withholding for 1998, and I certify that I meet **BOTH** of the following conditions for exemption:
- Last year I had a right to a refund of **ALL** Federal income tax withheld because I had **NO** tax liability **AND**
- This year I expect a refund of **ALL** Federal income tax withheld because I expect to have **NO** tax liability.

If you meet both conditions, enter "EXEMPT" here . . . . ▶ | **7**

Under penalties of perjury, I certify that I am entitled to the number of withholding allowances claimed on this certificate or entitled to claim exempt status.

Employee's signature ▶ _____ Date ▶ _____ , 19 ___

8 Employer's name and address (Employer: Complete 8 and 10 only if sending to the IRS)	**9** Office code (optional)	**10** Employer identification number

Cat. No. 10220Q

EMPLOYEE'S WITHHOLDING ALLOWANCE CERTIFICATE (W-4), p. 2

Write with a Group

*In groups of three, fill in the **Two-Earner/Two-Job Worksheet** using this information. • Report your amount on Line 9 to the class.*

1. This is a married couple. Both the husband and the wife had jobs in 1998.
2. Their number of exemptions on line H of page 1 is 8.
3. The husband's annual income was $22,400.
4. The wife's annual income was $37,000.
5. They completed this form in December, 1997.
6. They were not itemizing or claiming adjustments to income for 1998.

Two-Earner/Two-Job Worksheet

Note: *Use this worksheet only if the instructions for line H on page 1 direct you here.*

1. Enter the number from line H on page 1 (or from line 10 above if you used the Deductions and Adjustments Worksheet) ... **1** _____

2. Find the number in **Table 1** below that applies to the **LOWEST** paying job and enter it here ... **2** _____

3. If line 1 is **GREATER THAN OR EQUAL TO** line 2, subtract line 2 from line 1. Enter the result here (if zero, enter -0-) and on Form W-4, line 5, on page 1. **DO NOT** use the rest of this worksheet ... **3** _____

Note: *If line 1 is **LESS THAN** line 2, enter -0- on Form W-4, line 5, on page 1. Complete lines 4–9 to calculate the additional withholding amount necessary to avoid a year end tax bill.*

4. Enter the number from line 2 of this worksheet ... **4** _____
5. Enter the number from line 1 of this worksheet ... **5** _____
6. **Subtract** line 5 from line 4 ... **6** _____
7. Find the amount in **Table 2** below that applies to the **HIGHEST** paying job and enter it here ... **7** $ _____
8. **Multiply** line 7 by line 6 and enter the result here. This is the additional annual withholding amount needed ... **8** $ _____
9. Divide line 8 by the number of pay periods remaining in 1998. (For example, divide by 26 if you are paid every other week and you complete this form in December 1997.) Enter the result here and on Form W-4, line 6, page 1. This is the additional amount to be withheld from each paycheck ... **9** $ _____

Table 1: Two-Earner/Two-Job Worksheet

Married Filing Jointly				All Others			
If wages from **LOWEST** paying job are—	Enter on line 2 above	If wages from **LOWEST** paying job are—	Enter on line 2 above	If wages from **LOWEST** paying job are—	Enter on line 2 above	If wages from **LOWEST** paying job are—	Enter on line 2 above
0 - $4,000	0	38,001 - 43,000	8	0 - $5,000	0	70,001 - 85,000	8
4,001 - 7,000	1	43,001 - 54,000	9	5,001 - 11,000	1	85,001 - 100,000	9
7,001 - 12,000	2	54,001 - 62,000	10	11,001 - 16,000	2	100,001 and over	10
12,001 - 18,000	3	62,001 - 70,000	11	16,001 - 21,000	3		
18,001 - 24,000	4	70,001 - 85,000	12	21,001 - 25,000	4		
24,001 - 28,000	5	85,001 - 100,000	13	25,001 - 42,000	5		
28,001 - 33,000	6	100,001 - 110,000	14	42,001 - 55,000	6		
33,001 - 38,000	7	110,001 and over	15	55,001 - 70,000	7		

Table 2: Two-Earner/Two-Job Worksheet

Married Filing Jointly		All Others	
If wages from **HIGHEST** paying job are—	Enter on line 7 above	If wages from **HIGHEST** paying job are—	Enter on line 7 above
0 - $50,000	$400	0 - $30,000	$400
50,001 - 100,000	760	30,001 - 60,000	760
100,001 - 130,000	840	60,001 - 120,000	840
130,001 - 240,000	970	120,001 - 250,000	970
240,001 and over	1,070	250,001 and over	1,070

Cross-Cultural Exchange

Do people pay withholding tax in your country? • Are income taxes high or low in your country? • What percent of income do people pay for taxes?

REQUEST FOR EARNINGS AND BENEFIT ESTIMATE STATEMENT

Read with the Class

Study this Social Security ***Request for Earnings and Benefit Estimate Statement*** *together.* • *Discuss the vocabulary.*

Form Approved
OMB No. 0960-0466 ☐ SP

Request for Earnings and Benefit Estimate Statement

☐ Please check this box if you want to get your statement in Spanish instead of English.

Please print or type your answers. When you have completed the form, fold it and mail it to us.

1. Name shown on your Social Security card:

_____ _____
First Name   Middle Initial

_____
Last Name Only

2. Your Social Security number as shown on your card:

☐☐☐-☐☐-☐☐☐☐

3. Your date of birth _____ _____ _____
                       Month   Day   Year

4. Other Social Security numbers you have used:

☐☐☐-☐☐-☐☐☐☐
☐☐☐-☐☐-☐☐☐☐

5. Your sex: ☐ Male   ☐ Female

6. Other names you have used
(including a maiden name):

_____
_____

For items 7 and 9 show only earnings covered by Social Security. Do NOT include wages from State, local or Federal Government employment that are NOT covered for Social Security or that are covered ONLY by Medicare.

7. Show your actual earnings (wages and/or net self-employment income) for last year and your estimated earnings for this year.

A. Last year's actual earnings: *(Dollars Only)*

$ ☐☐☐,☐☐☐.☐0☐0

B. This year's estimated earnings: *(Dollars Only)*

$ ☐☐☐,☐☐☐.☐0☐0

8. Show the age at which you plan to stop working.

☐☐ *(Show only one age)*

9. Below, show the average yearly amount (not your total future lifetime earnings) that you think you will earn between now and when you plan to stop working. Include cost-of-living, performance or scheduled pay increases or bonuses.

If you expect to earn significantly more or less in the future due to promotions, job changes, part-time work, or an absence from the work force, enter the amount that most closely reflects your future average yearly earnings.

If you don't expect any significant changes, show the same amount you are earning now (the amount in 7B).

Future average yearly earnings: *(Dollars Only)*

$ ☐☐☐,☐☐☐.☐0☐0

10. Address where you want us to send the statement.

_____
Name

_____
Street Address (Include Apt. No., P.O. Box, or Rural Route)

_____
City   State   Zip Code

Notice:
I am asking for information about my own Social Security record or the record of a person I am authorized to represent. I understand that when requesting information on a deceased person, I must include proof of death and relationship or appointment. I further understand that if I deliberately request information under false pretenses , I may be guilty of a Federal crime and could be fined and/or imprisoned. I authorize you to use a contractor to send the statement of earnings and benefit estimates to the person named in item 10.

▶

_____
Please sign your name (Do Not Print)

_____   _____
Date   (Area Code) Daytime Telephone No.

Form SSA-7004-SM(4-95) Destroy prior editions   ♻ Printed on recycled paper

---

Print

Fill in your own information on the form.

Class Survey

"What is the best age to stop working?" • *Write your answer to the question.* • *Then survey your class.* • *Ask the same question.* • *Write the class results on the board.*

U.S. INCOME TAX RETURN

Class Brainstorm

Make a list on the board of kinds of income that people have to pay income tax on.

Read with the Class

*Study this **1040 EZ** United States Income Tax Form together.* • *Discuss the vocabulary.*

Department of the Treasury—Internal Revenue Service

Form 1040EZ

Income Tax Return for Single and Joint Filers With No Dependents (P)

OMB No. 1545-0675

Use the IRS label here

Your first name and initial   Last name

If a joint return, spouse's first name and initial   Last name

Home address (number and street). If you have a P.O. box, see page 7.   Apt. no.

City, town or post office, state, and ZIP code. If you have a foreign address, see page 7.

Presidential Election Campaign
(See page 7.)

Note: *Checking "Yes" will not change your tax or reduce your refund.*

Do you want $3 to go to this fund? ▶

If a joint return, does your spouse want $3 to go to this fund? ▶

Income

Attach Copy B of Form(s) W-2 here. Enclose, but do not attach, any payment with your return.

1 Total wages, salaries, and tips. This should be shown in box 1 of your W-2 form(s). Attach your W-2 form(s).   1

2 Taxable interest income of $400 or less. If the total is over $400, you cannot use Form 1040EZ.   2

3 Unemployment compensation (see page 9).   3

4 Add lines 1, 2, and 3. This is your **adjusted gross income**. If under $9,500, see page 9 to find out if you can claim the earned income credit on line 8.   4

Note: *You **must** check Yes or No.*

5 Can your parents (or someone else) claim you on their return?
Yes. Enter amount from worksheet on back.
No. If **single**, enter 6,550.00. If **married**, enter 11,800.00. See back for explanation.   5

6 Subtract line 5 from line 4. If line 5 is larger than line 4, enter 0. This is your **taxable income**. ▶ 6

Payments and tax

7 Enter your Federal income tax withheld from box 2 of your W-2 form(s).   7

8 **Earned income credit** (see page 9). Enter type and amount of nontaxable earned income below.
Type $ 8

9 Add lines 7 and 8 (do not include nontaxable earned income). These are your **total payments**.   9

10 **Tax.** Use the amount on **line 6** to find your tax in the tax table on pages 20–24 of the booklet. Then, enter the tax from the table on this line.   10

U.S. INCOME TAX RETURN, p. 2

Refund

Have it sent directly to your bank account! See page 13 and fill in 11b, c, and d.

11a If line 9 is larger than line 10, subtract line 10 from line 9. This is your **refund.**   11a

▶ **b** Routing number

▶ **c** Type   **d** Account number
     Checking   Savings

Amount you owe

12 If line 10 is larger than line 9, subtract line 9 from line 10. This is the **amount you owe.** See page 13 for details on how to pay and what to write on your payment.   12

I have read this return. Under penalties of perjury, I declare that to the best of my knowledge and belief, the return is true, correct, and accurately lists all amounts and sources of income I received during the tax year.

Sign here

Keep copy for your records.

Your signature   Spouse's signature if joint return

Date   Your occupation   Date   Spouse's occupation

For Official Use Only

For Privacy Act and Paperwork Reduction Act Notice, see page 5.   Cat. No. 12616G   Form 1040EZ

Print

*Now fill in your own information on this **1040 EZ** United States Income Tax Form.*

Cross-Cultural Exchange

Answer these questions with your class. • Write the answers on the board.

1. Are income tax forms similar to this in your country?
2. In what ways are they different?
3. Which do you prefer?

UNEMPLOYMENT

Cross-Cultural Exchange

Answer these questions with your class. • *Is there unemployment insurance in your country?* • *What happens when a person loses a job?*

Read with the Class

Study this form together. • *Discuss the vocabulary.* • *Answer the questions below.*

UB-105 (7-96)	ARIZONA DEPARTMENT OF ECONOMIC SECURITY

Employment Security Administration

ARIZONA INITIAL CLAIM FOR UNEMPLOYMENT INSURANCE

PRINT ONLY	DO NOT COMPLETE SHADED AREAS	BA-CLMT INFO

1. SOC. SEC. NO. 006-82-9765
28. SOC. SEC. VERIF. *FOR OFFICIAL USE ONLY*
29. DEPUTY NO.

2. LAST NAME Parker **FIRST NAME** Susan **MIDDLE INITIAL** E
30. ☐ BE

3. MAILING ADDRESS *(No., Street, Apt., P.O. Box, City)* 2140 Cactus Drive, Phoenix **STATE** AZ **ZIP** 85044
31. FIPS-RESIDENCE

4. RESIDENTIAL ADDRESS *(If different from mailing address)* **STATE** AZ **ZIP**
32. SEX **33. ETHNIC**

5. PHONE NO. (602) 759-1310 **6. OCCUPATION** retail salesclerk
34. W/H-FED **35. W/H-STA**

7. BIRTHDATE Month 10 Day 20 Year 67
8. OTHER NAMES OR SOC. SEC. NOS. YOU USED IN THE LAST TWO (2) YEARS
BB-CLAIM INFO
36. CIRCLE CLM ACTION N A R I

Yes No *Additional deputy action required
37. EFFECTIVE DATE

9. ☒ *☐ Are you a citizen of the United States?

☐ *☐ If not a citizen, were you legally authorized to work in the United States during the past 18 months? If Yes, Permit No. _____.
38. FILE DATE

10. ☐ ☒ Are you disabled? *(This information is voluntary and will be used for statistical purposes only.)*
39. LO **40. TYPE**

11. *☒ ☐ In the past 12 months have you filed an unemployment insurance claim in any state?

12. *☐ ☒ In the past 18 months have you been in the military service?

13. *☐ ☒ In the past 18 months have you worked in federal civilian service?
41. DISABILITY DATE

14. *☒ ☐ In the past 18 months have you worked in another state?

15. *☐ ☒ Are you currently working and filing this claim under the Shared Work Program?
42. NON-SEP ISSUES

16. *☒ ☐ Have you received or will you receive vacation, holiday, or unused sick pay from your employer?

17. *☐ ☒ Are you receiving or have you applied for Social Security retirement benefits or any other type of retirement, pension/annuity benefits?
43. JS REQ. **44. ERI** **45. P/F**

18. *☐ ☒ Have you refused work or referral to work since becoming unemployed?
46. REQ. CWC **47. SUPP DD** **48. WG PEND**

19. *☐ ☒ Since becoming unemployed have you received Workers' Compensation for a work-connected injury or disability?
BC-EMPLOYER INFO

20. ☐ ☒ Are you required to make or do you owe court-ordered child support payments?
49. EMPLOYER NO.

1. Who is filing this claim?

2. Where does she live?

3. How old is she?

4. What kind of work does she do?

5. What is her citizenship status?

6. What information will the deputy need to take additional action in her case?

UNEMPLOYMENT, p. 2

Print

Fill in the information for yourself.

UB-105 (7-96)	ARIZONA DEPARTMENT OF ECONOMIC SECURITY Employment Security Administration		

ARIZONA INITIAL CLAIM FOR UNEMPLOYMENT INSURANCE

PRINT ONLY	DO NOT COMPLETE SHADED AREAS	BA-CLMT INFO

1. SOC. SEC. NO.	28. SOC. SEC. VERIF.	*FOR OFFICIAL USE ONLY*	29. DEPUTY NO.

2. LAST NAME	FIRST NAME	MIDDLE INITIAL	30. ☐ BE

3. MAILING ADDRESS *(No., Street, Apt., P.O. Box, City)*	STATE AZ	ZIP	31. FIPS-RESIDENCE

4. RESIDENTIAL ADDRESS *(If different from mailing address)*	STATE AZ	ZIP	32. SEX	33. ETHNIC

5. PHONE NO.	6. OCCUPATION	34. W/H-FED	35. W/H-STA

7. BIRTHDATE Month	Day	Year	8. OTHER NAMES OR SOC. SEC. NOS. YOU USED IN THE LAST TWO (2) YEARS	BB-CLAIM INFO 36. CIRCLE CLM ACTION N A R I

Yes **No** ***Additional deputy action required**

	Yes	No		
9.	☐	*☐	Are you a citizen of the United States?	37. EFFECTIVE DATE
	☐	*☐	If not a citizen, were you legally authorized to work in the United States during the past 18 months? If Yes, Permit No. _____ .	38. FILE DATE
10.	☐	☐	Are you disabled? *(This information is voluntary and will be used for statistical purposes only.)*	
11.	*☐	☐	In the past 12 months have you filed an unemployment insurance claim in any state?	39. LO 40. TYPE
12.	*☐	☐	In the past 18 months have you been in the military service?	
13.	*☐	☐	In the past 18 months have you worked in federal civilian service?	41. DISABILITY DATE
14.	*☐	☐	In the past 18 months have you worked in another state?	
15.	*☐	☐	Are you currently working and filing this claim under the Shared Work Program?	42. NON-SEP ISSUES
16.	*☐	☐	Have you received or will you receive vacation, holiday, or unused sick pay from your employer?	
17.	*☐	☐	Are you receiving or have you applied for Social Security retirement benefits or any other type of retirement, pension/annuity benefits?	43. JS REQ. 44. ERI 45. P/F
18.	*☐	☐	Have you refused work or referral to work since becoming unemployed?	46. REQ. CWC 47. SUPP DD 48. WG PEND.
19.	*☐	☐	Since becoming unemployed have you received Workers' Compensation for a work-connected injury or disability?	BC-EMPLOYER INFO
20.	☐	☐	Are you required to make or do you owe court-ordered child support payments?	49. EMPLOYER NO.

Community Activity

Where is the local unemployment office? • Look it up in the telephone directory. • Find the name of your state and look under UNEMPLOYMENT. *• Write the address and the telephone number.*

Address   Telephone Number

_____   _____

_____

134

BUSINESS WRITING

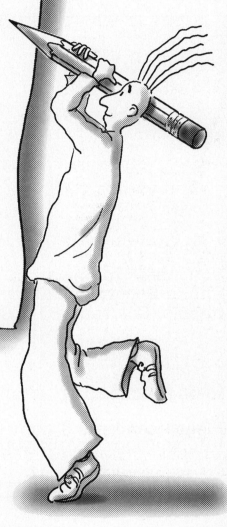

SPELLING HINT

➤ The **short u sound** is usually spelled letter **u**, **o**, or **ou**.

s**u**n	s**o**n	en**ou**gh
c**u**p	m**o**ther	th**ou**gh
under	m**o**ney	r**ou**gh

BUSINESS LETTER: REQUEST FOR INFORMATION

Read with the Class

Read this letter together.

19 Rainbow Drive
San Rafael, Texas 23445
October 4, 2000

Consumer Information
Public Documents Distribution Center
Pueblo, Colorado 81009

Dear Sir:

Please send me a copy of your free booklet, <u>Consumer
Information</u>. Thank you for your assistance.

Sincerely,

_____
(name)

Read with the Class

Read this list of consumer information sources together. • *Complete the list.*

1. *Write to ask for a copy of the pamphlet,* **Family Emergency Almanac.**

   The National Safety Council
   425 North Michigan Avenue
   Chicago, IL 60611

2. *Write to ask for the latest publications.*

   U.S. Consumer Product Safety Commission
   Washington, D.C. 20207

3. *Write to ask for a copy of the pamphlet* **Fly Rights,** *for information about passengers'
   rights on airlines.*

   The Civil Aeronautics Board
   Consumer Information Center
   Pueblo, CO 81009

4. *Look up the nearest address in your telephone directory.* • *Write the address on the lines.*
   • *Write to ask for information and a membership application.*

   American Automotive Association (AAA)

   _____

   _____

   _____

5. *Look up the address in your telephone directory under the name of your state.* • *Write to
   ask for a list of the public recreational facilities in your state.*

   Parks and Recreation Division (your state)

   _____

   _____

   _____

Write with a Partner   Partner's Name _____

Choose one of these consumer information sources. • *Write a letter for information.* • *Read
your letter to the class.* • *Then mail the letter.* • *Bring the information to class when you
receive it.*

COLLEGE INFORMATION REQUEST

Community Activity

If you want to know more about a college or university, ask a school counselor or go to the library. • *Write the name and address of the school you are interested in.* • *Bring the information to class and write it on the board.*

Write

Write this letter to request information.

_____ (1)

_____

_____ (2)

Admissions Office

_____ (3)

_____ (4)

_____

Dear Sir:

I am currently attending _____ (5)

_____ . I am interested in

applying to _____ (3)

to study _____ (6) .

Please send me a catalog, an application for

admission, and information regarding financial aid.

Thank you.

     Sincerely,

    _____ (7)

1. Your address
2. Today's date
3. Name of school you are writing to
4. School's address
5. Name of your school
6. Major subject area
7. Your signature

Write with a Partner   Partner's Name _____

With a partner, write a telephone conversation between a prospective student and a college admissions officer. • *Ask for information and an application.* • *Give your name and address.* • *Read your conversation to the class.*

138

CLASSIFIED ADS

Read with the Class

Read these advertisements together. • What is for sale? • What are the prices? • What should you do to get more information?

CLASSIFIED	CLASSIFIED
GARAGE SALE – NEW CITY Everything must go! Sat. and Sun. 9-4. 56 Woodland Ave.	**LIKE NEW** – Refrigerator, freezer, washer, dryer, stove. $75 each. 908-555-8462 eve.
MOVING – Full size BR set, LR set & refrig, microwave, washing machine, color TV. 908-555-2349	**PRINTER** – Macintosh HP Deskwriter Printer, Exc. cond. – Asking $125 Call Maria after 5pm 908-555-6545
POOL TABLE–99" HAWTHORNE By Brunswick. Good cond. $500 FIRM. Call 718-555-7899	**3 pc Liv Rm SET** – incs sofa bed & 2 wingbk chrs. Beige, Shwrm cond. Ask'g $725 also sold sep. 908-555-6645 aft. 11 am lve msg.
PIANO – Fruitwood Baby Grand. A steal at $4500. Call 973-555-9789	

Write with the Class

List all the abbreviations from these ads on the board. • What do they mean? • Write the complete word for each abbreviation.

Write with a Group

In groups of three, decide which items in these ads you would like to buy. • Circle the ads. • Write a telephone conversation with the person who is selling each item. • Read your conversations to the class.

Write with a Partner   Partner's Name _____

With a partner, write a newspaper ad for something you want to sell. • Read your ad to the class.

Class Project

Run a yard sale with your class. • Write an ad for your yard sale. • Submit the ad to a local newspaper.

CAR ADS

Read with the Class

Read these car ads together. • *What are the prices?* • *Which ones look interesting to you?* • *Why?*

CARS	**TRUCKS AND VANS**
1993 Corolla – 4 dr, 5 spd stick. Air-bag, A/C, AM/FM cass, exc. cond, 65k mi, $10,000. 555-5962	1985 FORD F350 – Tow truck, heavy duty, 120k, asking $3700 OBO. Call Jim at 555-7240
1971 VW BEETLE – 90k, looks and runs great. $1750 or best offer. Call 701-555-6989	1996 DODGE RAM 1500 4x4 – Fully loaded, w/ snow plow, 23k miles, $15,000 Firm. 555-9812
'87 SAAB 900S-Silver, 3dr HB, 5spd, a/c, lovingly maint. $3300. 974-555-9225	1990 FORD CONVERSION VAN – CD player, TV, Bed, Absolutely mint. Loaded $5900. Must Sell! Call Juan 291-555-1495
1988 CHEVY CAVALIER – 4 dr, wag. Auto/AC, ps, pb, mint cond. $2800 or best offer. 712-555-8426	1987 TOYOTA 4x4, Deluxe long bed pick-up. Call 732-555-4657

Write with the Class

List all the abbreviations from these ads on the board. • *What do they mean?* • *Write the complete word for each abbreviation.*

Group Game: Sell a Car

In groups of three, write an ad to sell a car. • *Then give your ad to another group.* • *Talk with the other group about your ad.* • *Convince them to buy your car.*

Community Activity

Bring in the car ads from your newspaper. • *Write all the abbreviations from the ads on the board.* • *Write the complete word for each abbreviation.* • *Would you like to buy any of the cars?* • *Which ones?*

MAIL ORDER

Read with your Class

Read this order form together. • *What is this order for?*

1 Ordered By:
SUSAN ROE
102 RICHMOND AVE
LITTLETON, CO 80135

3 Payment Method: ☐ Credit Card (check one):
☐ Check or Money Order
(payable to Health Corner)
Credit Card Number:

☐ ☐   ☐ ☐

_ _ _ _ -- _ _ _ _ -- _ _ _ _ -- _ _ _ _

Exp. Date: _____ Signature: _____

4 Daytime Phone Number: _____
(In case we have any questions regarding your order.)

2 Please Print Details of Your Order:

Item No.	Item Description	Size	Quantity	Each Price	Extension

Shipping & Handling Charge (Add $1.00 for each additional delivery address.)		
Up to $10.00	$ 3.50
$10.01 - 20.00	$ 4.50
$20.01 - 30.00	$ 5.50
$30.01 - 40.00	$ 6.50
$40.01 - 50.00	$ 7.50
$50.01 - 70.00	$ 8.50
Over $70.00	$10.50

Total Merchandise	
Delivery & Handling	
Optional Express Delivery	
Total Amount Enclosed	

5 If paying by check or money order, insert in pocket below, fold and seal. *Thank you for your order*

Write with a Partner   Partner's Name _____

With a partner, choose two items below that you want to order. • *Fill in the catalog order form for each item.*

- (S-27077-5) Men's long-sleeved cotton *Wild Man* sweatshirt, S/M/L/XL/XXL, navy/burgundy/grey, $15.99 (2 for $25.00)
- (LX-3914-6) Women's fleece-lined slippers, sizes 4-10, white/tan/light blue, $11.99
- Beach towel: (B-14680-X) jungle print, (B-14681-X) football, (B-14682-X) tropical fish, $8.49
- (S-70833-PR) Woven leather belt with silver buckle, Women's: S/M/L, Men's S/M/L/XL, brown/black/tan, $18.95.

Community Activity

Bring a mail order catalog to class. • *Explain your catalog to the class.* • *Show what you would like to order from the catalog.*

Write with a Partner   Partner's Name _____

With a partner, write a conversation between a telephone customer and a telephone sales representative to order your catalog items. • *Read your conversation to the class.*

RETURNING MERCHANDISE

Read with the Class

Read this letter together to return merchandise. • *Add more choices for reasons to return merchandise.*

Write

Complete this letter.

_____ (1)

_____

_____ (2)

_____ (3)

_____ (4)

_____

Dear Sir:

Last week I received the _____ (5)

_____ that I purchased. I

am returning it with this letter because

_____ (6)

_____ .

Thank you.

Sincerely,

_____ (7)

1. Your address
2. Today's date
3. Name of company
4. Address of company
5. Item you are going to return
6. Choose one:
   • *it arrived broken*
   • *there are pieces missing*
   • *it doesn't fit*
   • *I don't like the color*
   • *other:*

   _____

7. Your name

Write with a Partner

Partner's Name _____

With a partner, decide on an item you have bought by mail and want to return. • *Complete the letter to return your merchandise.* • *Read your letter to the class.*

COMPLAINT ABOUT A BILLING ERROR

Write

With your class, add more choices. • ***Then complete the letter.***

_____ (1)

_____

_____ (2)

ITL Company
Billing Department
Box 82
Danvers, Massachusetts 01923

Dear Sir or Madam:

There is an error in the bill I have just received.

_____ (3)

_____.

(See enclosed copy of bill.) Please investigate and correct this situation. Thank you.

Yours truly,

_____ (4)

1. Your address
2. Today's date
3. Choose one:
   - *I paid this bill last month*
   - *I did not purchase the item circled*
   - *I returned the circled item several weeks ago*
   - *This is the third month I have requested this correction*
   - *other:*

   _____

4. Your signature

Write

You received a monthly bill from the gas company for $500. • *Write a letter.* • *Explain the error.* • *Ask for a corrected bill.*

Group Brainstorm

In groups of three, decide how to follow-up your letter. • *List all possibilities.* • *Read your list to the class.*

FREE OFFERS

Community Activity

What is junk mail? • *Bring free offer forms and other junk mail to class.* • *Be careful!* • *Do the offers really say what you think they do?*

Write

Which of these offers would you prefer to have? • *Fill out the one you want.*

FREE CARRIBEAN CRUISE

☐ Yes, tell me if I am the winner of the all-expense paid Carribean Cruise for two. Please send me a full year of *Travel Journal*—12 idea-packed issues for only $12. **I SAVE $11.88 off the cover price!**

☐ No, I'll give up my $11.88 savings. Just enter me in the sweepstakes.

Please print

Name _____

Address _____ Apt. # _____

City _____ State _____ Zip _____

SEND NO MONEY—We'll bill you later!

THIS OFFER EXPIRES

MAY 15, 2002

TRAVEL JOURNAL

MAIL TODAY • MAIL TODAY • MAIL TODAY • MAIL TODAY • MAIL TODAY

Improve your Appearance.

Choose from our many different styles:

Order your FREE wig catalog and you may win a FREE wig

"I love my wigs. They let me change my look in seconds...there are no more bad hair days!"

For a FREE catalog and a chance to win a FREE wig, send this card today.
No cost or obligation. Nothing to buy.

Name _____

Address _____

City _____ State _____ Zip _____

How often do you wear wigs?
❏ Almost every day   ❏ Once or twice a week
❏ Sometimes   ❏ Never

Class Game: Win a Cruise! Win a Wig!

Write your name on a slip of paper. • *Fold the paper.* • *Make a pile.* • *Pick the winners!*

CANCELLING A SUBSCRIPTION

Class Survey

Survey the class. • How many have a subscription? • List all the subscriptions on the board. • Include subscriptions to record/CD clubs, book clubs, video clubs, magazines, etc. • What are good reasons to cancel a subscription? • Has anyone ever cancelled a subscription? • Tell why.

Write

With your class, add more choices. • Complete the letter to cancel a subscription.

_____ (1)
_____
_____ (2)

Subscription Department
WEEKLY MAGAZINE
Box 8382
Columbia, MO 65205

Dear Sir:
Please cancel my subscription to WEEKLY MAGAZINE. Since I have _____ (3)
_____ , please
_____ (4)
_____ .

Sincerely,

_____ (5)

1. Your address
2. Today's date
3. Choose one:
   - *paid in advance*
   - *returned last week's copy*
   - *not signed up for this year*
   - *other:*

   _____

4. Choose one:
   - *return my payment*
   - *return the balance of my payments*
   - *do not send me any further copies*
   - *other:*

   _____

5. Your signature

Write with a Partner   Partner's Name _____

With a partner, choose a subscription to cancel. • Write a letter to cancel the subscription. • Read your letter to another pair of students.

Class Project

Bring in magazines and books you would like to share with your classmates. • Start a lending library or an exchange. • Have a sign-out sheet.

FLIP SIDES

➤ Choose one Flip Side sheet to copy on the back of each lesson.

➤ Use the Flip Side to provide for more writing.

Business Letter

_____

_____

_____

_____

_____

_____

_____

_____

_____

_____

_____

_____

_____

_____

_____

_____

Name: _____

Date: _____

Class: _____

Teacher: _____

Directions

_____

_____

_____

_____

_____

_____

_____

_____

_____

_____

_____

_____

_____

_____

_____

_____

Name: _____

Date: _____

Class: _____

Teacher: _____

Journal

_____

_____

_____

_____

_____

_____

_____

_____

_____

_____

_____

_____

_____

_____

_____

_____

_____

_____

Name: _____

Date: _____

Class: _____

Teacher: _____

List

1. _____
2. _____
3. _____
4. _____
5. _____
6. _____
7. _____
8. _____
9. _____
10. _____
11. _____
12. _____
13. _____
14. _____
15. _____
16. _____
17. _____
18. _____
19. _____
20. _____

Name: _____

Date: _____

Class: _____

Teacher: _____

Listen and Write

1. _____
2. _____
3. _____
4. _____
5. _____
6. _____
7. _____
8. _____
9. _____
10. _____
11. _____
12. _____
13. _____
14. _____
15. _____
16. _____
17. _____
18. _____
19 _____
20. _____

Name: _____

Date: _____

Class: _____

Teacher: _____

Partner Interview

_____

_____

_____

_____

_____

_____

_____

_____

_____

_____

_____

_____

_____

_____

_____

_____

_____

Name: _____

Date: _____

Class: _____

Teacher: _____

Personal Letter

_____

_____

_____

_____

_____

_____

_____

_____

_____

_____

_____

_____

_____

_____

Name: _____

Date: _____

Class: _____

Teacher: _____

Review

_____

_____

_____

_____

_____

_____

_____

_____

_____

_____

_____

_____

_____

_____

_____

_____

_____

Name: _____

Date: _____

Class: _____

Teacher: _____

Vocabulary

Word   **Meaning**

_____   _____

_____   _____

_____   _____

_____   _____

_____   _____

_____   _____

_____   _____

_____   _____

_____   _____

_____   _____

_____   _____

_____   _____

_____   _____

_____   _____

Name: _____

Date: _____

Class: _____

Teacher: _____

Weekly Planner

Sunday: _____

_____

_____

Monday: _____

_____

_____

Tuesday: _____

_____

_____

Wednesday: _____

_____

_____

Thursday: _____

_____

_____

Friday: _____

_____

_____

Saturday: _____

_____

_____

Name: _____

Date: _____

Class: _____

Teacher: _____

_____

_____

_____

_____

_____

_____

_____

_____

_____

_____

_____

_____

_____

_____

_____

_____

_____

Name: _____

Date: _____

Class: _____

Teacher: _____